The Ponytail Girls

Escape From
Camp Porcupine

LEGACY PRESS

Other books in
The Ponytail Girls series:

Book 1
Meet the Ponytail Girls

Book 2
The Impossible Christmas Present

Book 3
Lost on Monster Mountain

Book 4
A Stormy Spring

Book 6
What's Up With Her?

The Ponytail Girls

Escape From Camp Porcupine

Bonnie Compton Hanson

Dedication

For the wonderful women each of you
will become as you ask God to guide you.

THE PONYTAIL GIRLS/BOOK 5: ESCAPE FROM CAMP PORCUPINE
©2004 by Legacy Press, fourth printing
ISBN 1-58411-033-3
Legacy reorder# LP48045

Legacy Press
P.O. Box 261129
San Diego, CA 92196

Illustrator: Aline Heiser

Scriptures are from the *Holy Bible: New International Version*
(North American Edition), ©1973, 1978, 1984 by the
International Bible Society. Used by permission of
Zondervan Bible Publishers.

Printed in the United States of America

Contents

~ Introduction ~

Welcome to the Ponytail Girls! Whether you wear a ponytail or not you can share in the adventures of Sam Pearson and her friends, the PTs (that's short for Ponytails!). Just like you, the PTs love sports and shopping and fun with their friends at school.

The PTs also want to live in a way that is pleasing to God. So when they have problems and conflicts, they look to God and His Word, the Bible. They might also seek help from their parents, their pastor or their Sunday school class teacher, just like you do.

Each chapter in this book presents a new problem for your PTs to solve. Then there is a Bible story to help explain the Christian value that the PTs learned. A Bible memory verse is included for you to practice and share.

There may be words in this book that are new to you, especially some Bible names and Spanish words. Look them up in the Glossary on page 189, then use the syllables to sound out the words.

In addition to the stories, in each chapter you will find questions to answer and fun quizzes, puzzles and other activities. Also, at the end of each chapter starting with Chapter 1, you will get a clue that leads to finishing the Signs of the Times Puzzle on page 26. Don't forget to fill in the puzzle so you can see the secret message! The answers to all the puzzles (not that you'll need them!) are on page 191.

The first *Ponytail Girls* book, *Meet the Ponytail Girls*, began just before school started in the fall. In *The Impossible Christmas Present*, you followed the PTs through the tragedies and triumphs of their holiday season. *Lost on Monster Mountain* saw the PTs off to Winter Camp with their Madison classmates. *A Stormy Spring* followed the PTs' adventures during the rest of the school year. Now school's out. Let the summer fun begin!

The fun doesn't end with the stories. You can start your own Ponytail Girls Club. You can join by yourself, of course. But its much more fun if one of your friends joins with you. Or even five or six of them! There is no cost. You can read the Ponytail Girls stories together, do the puzzles and other activities, study the Bible stories and learn the Bible verses.

If your friends each have their own *Ponytail Girls* books, you can all write in yours at the same time. Arrange a regular meeting time and place and plan to do special things together, just like the PTs do in the stories, such as shopping, Bible study, homework, or helping others.

Meet Your Ponytail Girls!

• WHO ARE THEY? •

The Ponytail Girls are girls your age who enjoy school, church, shopping and being with their friends and family. They also love meeting new friends. Friends just like you! You will like being a part of their lives.

The PTs all attend Madison Middle School in the small town of Circleville. They're all also members of Miss Kotter's Sunday school class at nearby Faith Church on Sunday mornings. On Sunday evenings, they attend the special Zone 56 youth group for guys and girls their age. Their pastor is Rev. J. T. McConahan, and their youth leader is Pastor Andrew Garretti, whom they call "Pastor Andy."

Sam and Sara grew up in Circleville. Le's and LaToya's families moved into their neighborhood last year. When Sam and Sara met them at school, they invited them to church. Then Maria moved to Circleville and she became a PT, followed by Jenna and Sonya. Now it would be hard for all seven of them to imagine not being PTs!

How did the PTs get their club name? Well, as you can see from their pictures, they all wear a ponytail of one kind or another. So that's what their other friends and families started calling them just for fun.

Then one day LaToya shortened it to "PTs." Now that's what they all call themselves!

The PTs' club meetings are held whenever they can all get together. The girls have a secret motto: PT4JC, which means "Ponytails for Jesus Christ." They also have a secret code for the club's name: a "P" and a "T" back to back. But most of the time they don't want to keep secrets. They want to share with everyone the Good News about their best friend, Jesus.

Have fun sharing in your PTs' adventures. Laugh with them in their silly time, think and pray with them through their problems. And learn with them that the answers to all problems can be found right in God's Word. Keep your Bible and a sharpened pencil handy. Sam and the others are waiting for you!

GET TO KNOW THE PTs

Sam Pearson *has a long blond ponytail, sparkling blue eyes and a dream: she wants to play professional basketball. She also likes to design clothes. Sam's name is really "Samantha," but her friends and family just call her "Sam" for short. Sam's little brother, Petie, is 7. Joe, her dad, is great at fixing things, like cars and bikes. Her mom, Jean, bakes scrumptious cakes and pies and works at the Paws and Pooches Animal Shelter. Sneezit is the family dog.*

LaToya Thomas' *black curls are ponytailed high above her ears. That way she doesn't miss a thing going on! LaToya's into gymnastics and playing the guitar. Her big sister, Tina, is in college, training to be a nurse. Her mom is a school teacher; her dad works nights at a supermarket. Also living with the Thomases is LaToya's beloved, wheelchair-bound grandmother, Granny B.*

13

Le Tran *parts her glossy black hair to one side, holding it back with one small ponytail. She loves sewing, soccer and playing the violin. Her mother, Viola, a concert pianist, often plays duets with her. Her father, Daniel, died in an accident. Mr. Tran became a Christian before he died. Le's mother was a Buddhist, but she became a Christian last year.*

Sara Fields *lives down the street from Sam. She keeps her fiery, red hair from flying away by tying it into a ponytail flat against each side of her head. Sara has freckles, glasses and a great sense of humor. She loves to sing. She also loves softball, ice skating and cheerleading. Sara has a big brother, Tony, and a big dog, Tank. Both her parents are artists.*

14

When **Maria Moreno** *moved in next door to Sam in September, she became the fifth PT. Maria pulls part of her long, brown hair into one topknot ponytail at the back; the rest hangs loose. She is tall, the way basketball-lover Sam would like to be! But Maria's into science, not basketball. At home, she helps her mother take care of her 6-year-old twin brothers, Juan and Ricardo, and a little sister, Lolita. The Morenos all speak Spanish as well as English.*

·Maria Moreno·

·Miss Kotter·

Miss Kitty Kotter, *the girls' Sunday school teacher, is not a PT, but she is an important part of their lives both in church and out of church. Miss Kotter works as a computer engineer. She also loves to go on hikes. Miss Kotter calls the Bible her "how-to book" because, she says, it tells "how to" live. Miss Kotter volunteers at the Circleville Rescue Mission.*

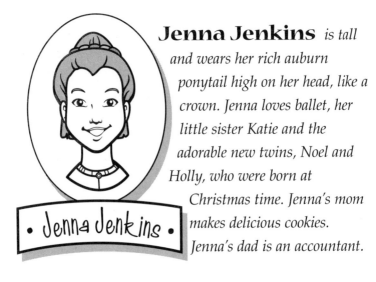

Jenna Jenkins *is tall and wears her rich auburn ponytail high on her head, like a crown. Jenna loves ballet, her little sister Katie and the adorable new twins, Noel and Holly, who were born at Christmas time. Jenna's mom makes delicious cookies. Jenna's dad is an accountant.*

Sonya Silverhorse *is disabled and uses a wheelchair. She has a sweet smile. Her bouncy cocker spaniel's name is Cocky. Sonya wears her coal-black ponytail long and braided in honor of her Cherokee background. She and her dad are new in town. He is Mr. Moreno's and Mr. Pearson's new boss. Her mother died in the accident that disabled Sonya.*

The newest PT is **Brittany Boorsma**. *Brittany, Madison's head cheerleader, has always been the prettiest and most spiteful girl at school. She pulls her long, naturally wavy blond hair together into a ponytail at her shoulder. Last winter, when her parents decided to separate, she was so upset she decided to kill herself, but she was rescued at the last minute. After that, Brittany made a decision to invite Christ into her life. Now she's trying hard to live for Him, just as the other PTs do.*

• Brittany Boorsma •

Get ready for fun with the PTs!

Chapter 1

School's Out!

The last couple of weeks of school zipped by so busy and fast that they seemed like a blur. First there was the Spring Concert, then Open House and the Art Show, followed by Memorial Day weekend, final class reports and exams.

"I feel like I'm on a roller coaster!" Sam Pearson gasped one day as she walked home from school with another Ponytail Girl, Maria Moreno. "A roller coaster without brakes! And without an end!"

But soon after, it was suddenly all over.

"School's out, school's out, Teacher's let the monkeys out!" shouted her little brother, Petie, as he rushed home the last day of school. He ran into the living room, threw his backpack onto the floor and turned on a cartoon full-blast. Then he ran outside with their dog, Sneezit, and dashed back in the door again, slamming the screen door behind him.

"School's out, Sam!" he yelled.

Sam grabbed the remote and turned off the TV. "Duh, Petie, I know — it's out for me, too. I sure am ready for a fun summer, too. Here, put your backpack away so Mom doesn't come home to a mess, okay? Want a snack?"

She slathered peanut butter and jelly onto slices of bread and poured two glasses of milk. "Now, tell me..."

But just then the twins Juan and Ricardo Moreno, Maria's brothers from next door, ran over.

"School's out!" they shouted.

Petie grinned. "I know. Want a sandwich?"

"Yeah!" Juan cried. Then, remembering his manners, he said, "I mean, yes, please."

After Sam made two more sandwiches for the twins, all three boys grabbed their snacks and rushed outside to the tree house. They took little Sneezit up with them.

Sam had just started biting into her own sandwich when the twins' little sister peeked in the front door. "School's out!" Lolita called.

Sam sighed. "Yes, I know, Lolita. Isn't it great? Would you like a sandwich, too?"

"Oh, thank you."

Handing her young visitor a sandwich, Sam asked, "Want to go eat it in the tree house with the boys?"

Lolita's face fell. "They won't let me. They put up a big sign that says, 'Boys only. Girls keep out.' "

"Then maybe you can play with Suzie or Katie. Suzie should be here any minute. I'm babysitting her after school today." Suzie was Sam's cousin, and Katie was Jenna Jenkins' little sister.

Lolita jumped up. "Really? Oh, great!"

After Suzie and Katie arrived, the little girls built a big "playhouse" in the backyard made from "walls" of lawn furniture. They filled it with the dolls and other toys they had brought with them. By the designated front door they put up a big, hand-lettered sign: "Girls only. Boys keep out."

After a while, two PTs, LaToya Thomas and Maria, stopped by. They helped  Sam make a pitcher of lemonade for everyone. LaToya took the pitcher and some plastic cups out to the boys' clubhouse and to the girls' tea party. Then the PTs sprawled out in Sam's family room with their own glasses of cool lemonade.

"Summertime!" LaToya sighed happily. "Three whole months with nothing to do!"

"Well, actually, two and a half," Sam reminded her.

"And we have lots to do," Maria added. "Jenna and I will be taking tennis lessons down at Shawnee Park. Plus Pastor Andy's been talking about Le and me helping out at the Midland church this summer. They're going to be having a VBS and busing in the migrant workers' children for it. In between, I promised to help Mama with stuff. Like washing the windows and weeding her garden."

"I'm volunteering at Whispering Pines," LaToya said. "Granny B.'s going with me. Plus I'm taking a gymnastics class. And I've got yard duty for our house and Mrs. Greenleaf's, too! What about you, Sam?"

Sam tried to keep it all straight. "Well, I'm taking a beginning sewing and design class. Le and her mom are going to help me on stuff 'cause they're so good at it. And the teacher said to bring any sketches we have of designs, too. So Mrs. Moreno is going to watch Petie and Suzie most of the time this summer, but sometimes I'm going to do it. Plus I have to take Petie to ball practice."

"Don't forget summer church camp," LaToya reminded her. "You know, at Camp Porcupine."

Sam pulled out her calendar and checked it. "Oops! I did forget. Wow, we might not have time to even do everything we want before school starts again!"

Just then they heard loud arguing and barking outside. Hurrying out, the girls discovered a shouting match: boys vs. girls. "Girls are stupid!" the boys taunted. "We can do anything better than you!"

"Boys are stupid!" the girls chanted back. "We can do anything better than you!"

"No, you can't!"

"Yes, we can!"

When they saw the older girls, they argued even louder.

"Sam," Suzie cried, "girls are better than boys, aren't they?"

Before Sam had a chance to answer her, Suzie's dad, who was also Sam's Uncle Todd, stopped by to pick up Suzie. He had a big bag in his arms.

"Uncle Todd," Petie argued, "boys are better than girls, aren't they?"

Uncle Todd looked at the boys and then he looked at the girls. "Well," he said, "guess what? I stopped by the store on the way over here for stuff to celebrate the first day of summer vacation." Then he emptied out packages of balloons, bottles of bubbles, whistles, bags of popcorn and party hats.

"I'd say the side that can enjoy all of this the most wins. Wouldn't you?" he said as he winked knowingly at the PTs.

Of course, the little boys and girls took the bait. As they dove into the goodies, they seemed to forget their "differences." When Uncle Todd said it was time for everyone to get home for dinner, they even helped each other clean up.

"Thanks, Uncle Todd," Sam said with a tired sigh. And this is only the first day of vacation, she thought. Hope it all works out this well!

· Good News · from God's Word

Who's better: boys or girls? The kids in Sam's backyard aren't the only ones in the world who argue about that. Many cultures think only sons are valuable and girls aren't important. In other cultures, people think girls are the most important because they can be sold for a lot of money. Let's see what God's Word has to say about it!

Ahlai Solves a Problem

FROM 1 CHRONICLES 2:31-35

In Bible times, land and other property were always inherited by the sons, usually the oldest son. The only time it could be inherited by a daughter was when the family had no sons. That's what happened to Naomi's family when her sons died. It is also what happened to the family of Mahlah and her four sisters, because they had no brothers.

This happened to another family as well — to a man named Sheshan.

Sheshan was wealthy. He had at least one servant, an Egyptian named Jarha. This servant was not wealthy like his master. He may have even been a slave. But he was a good worker and Sheshan considered him one of his family. Jarha was probably in charge of much of his master's affairs. In those days, if a master died without a son or heir, such a servant usually inherited everything.

Sheshan didn't have a son. But he did have a daughter named Ahlai. Which would have been better for Sheshan to do: give everything to Ahlai because he loved her? Or give everything to Jarha because he was such a good worker?

Actually, he was able to do both. Because Ahlai and Jarha decided to marry each other! That way, everything stayed in the family. Including a lot of love!

 ## A Verse to Remember

Blessed are the peacemakers.

— *Matthew 5:9*

What About You?

Have you ever been teased for being a girl? Write about it here:

_____

_____

Have you ever made fun of a brother or cousin or friend because they are boys? Write about that here:

_____

_____

Who made both women and men? And boys and girls? And loves them all? God, of course! Never be ashamed that you are a girl. You are God's princess!

But don't forget, God loves boys, too. They are His princes. You are all wonderful in His sight!

Signs of the Times Puzzle

Many people take vacation trips in the summer. The puzzle on the next page is full of signs on the highway to life. To solve this puzzle, write in the blanks the Secret Letters you will find at the end of each chapter in this book. For this chapter, write the letter "S" for "seeking peace" in space 5. The final solution is on page 191.

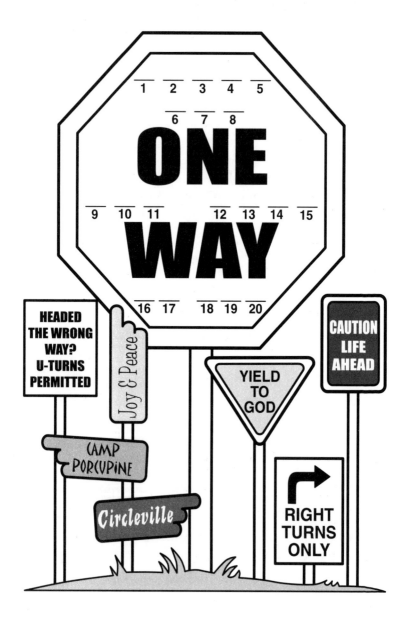

ONE WAY

1 2 3 4 5
6 7 8
9 10 11 12 13 14 15
16 17 18 19 20

HEADED THE WRONG WAY? U-TURNS PERMITTED

Joy & Peace

CAMP PORCUPINE

Circleville

YIELD TO GOD

CAUTION LIFE AHEAD

RIGHT TURNS ONLY

Chapter 2

Birthdays and Babies

GOOD LUCK RIC

While her parents attended a Christian marriage enrichment seminar over the weekend, Brittany stayed at Jenna's. On Saturday morning they helped Jenna's mom get ready for Katie's birthday party. Katie was turning 7. And Jenna's twin sisters,

Noel and Holly, were now six months old.

"Six months! Can you believe it?" Maria exclaimed at Shawnee Park later that day. In addition to Katie's friends, all of the PTs, their families and their dogs had been invited to her birthday party. The park was alive with balloons, banners and kids.

Noel could say, "Da-da-da-da-da." Holly could say, "Ma-ma-ma-ma-ma." They could also sit up now. They couldn't crawl yet, but they tried. Both had bright, golden-red curls that Jenna had pulled into tiny ponytails on the tops of their heads, like miniature genies. Sam was sure she had never seen anything as adorable in her entire life.

"I got to dress them this morning," Brittany said as she playfully tweaked Noel's ponytail.

Jenna laughed. "Yeah, but right after you dressed them, they spit up so Mom had to dress them all over again!"

Everyone took turns romping with their dogs in the nearby Bark Park. Then they put leashes on the dogs and brought them over to join the birthday party. Brittany's dogs, Sweetie and Hope, tried to "kiss" everyone they met, including the birthday girl and the baby twins. They especially tried to kiss the birthday cake frosting off the twins' faces.

"I really need to get them some obedience training," Brittany sighed. "But I don't know where to start."

"The animal shelter is going to have a class for

dogs this summer," Sam replied. Sam's mom worked at the Paws and Pooches Shelter. "Maybe you can sign up Sweetie and Hope."

Petie made a face. "That's not fair! We get the summer off from schools. The dogs should get it off, too!"

Miss Kitty, the PTs' Sunday school teacher, arrived a bit later than everyone else, but she had just as much fun. Inspired from watching the babies, she called for a hands-and-knees-only race across the grass.

Even Mr. Silverhorse entered the race. "Hey," he joked, "back where we used to live, the traffic on the freeway often slowed to a crawl. So I've had plenty of experience with this!"

The racing "babies" laughed so hard that some collapsed in a heap of giggles. Others pushed on — and Suzie won. As she sucked her thumb and crawled back to the party she yelled, "See what a big baby I am!"

Just about the time everyone was ready to go home, someone one else showed up. Someone who hadn't even been invited. Ric Romero!

He had a big package in his arms. "I'm glad I found you all," he said. "I wanted to give Katie a present while we're still in town. Now that school's out, Uncle Max and I are moving to Summer City for his new job. Tomorrow's our last day in Circleville." Handing his gift to Katie, he added, "Happy birthday, Katie!"

"Oooo!" she squealed. Ripping open the paper, she discovered a cuddly toy sheep.

"When I saw it in the store, I thought of me and Uncle Max being black sheep," Ric explained, blushing. "But now we both belong to God." He chuckled as he added, "Maybe our wool is still rough around the edges, but at least now we're in the right flock."

The next day at church, both Ric and his uncle came forward at the end of the service to make a public profession of faith. Everyone prayed for them. Le's mom, Mrs. Tran, offered to take them out to lunch afterward, but they said they were too busy packing.

"But I will be there for Zone 56 tonight," Ric said.

That afternoon, the PTs and other Zone 56 members quickly planned a going-away party for Ric.

"Ric, you've got to come back and visit a lot," Sonya insisted as she handed him a slice of Sam's mom's delicious cake. Sam had drawn a picture of Ric on the cake — complete with his former purple hair! — using icing.

Kevin nodded. "And play in our praise band."

"Oh, I will," he agreed. "And I'll see all you guys at Camp Porcupine, right? It's funny, as much as I hate to leave here, I feel like God is watching over us and sending us to a good place."

"Amen, brother!" said Pastor Andy with a smile. "And speaking of Camp Porcupine…it will be held the second week in August in the same part of the park where you went for Winter Camp. The church will help pay part of everyone's costs, but each of you will still need to come up with $75 for the rest. So you'd better start right now earning some money. Here are some fliers about it to take home to your parents."

As everyone got ready to leave, the girls hugged Ric good-bye. The guys gave him high-fives.

"See you at the wheelchair tournament in Summer City next month," he said to Sonya. "Bet you win the basketball game, hands down!"

"Hands down?" she protested with a laugh. "Then how could I get the ball in the basket?"

"Bye, Ric," said Maria. *Vaya con Dios.*

Ric grinned. "You know it, Maria!"

· Good News · from God's Word

Before they became Christians, Ric and his Uncle Max wanted nothing to do with God. Here is a Bible story about a young girl who was totally against God, too. Then God did something to change her life!

A Young Fortuneteller Meets a Man of God

FROM ACTS 16:16-21

As Paul traveled around telling people about God, he came to the bustling city of Corinth. There he met Lydia and some other women. When these women heard the Gospel of Jesus, they believed in Him right away.

"Come stay at my house while you preach

here," Lydia said.

So Paul and his friends stayed with her.

Because there were few Jews or Christians in that city, the people who wanted to worship God met together under the trees by the riverbank. That's where Paul had met Lydia. So one day he and his friend Silas went there again to worship with believers.

But they ran into a problem. Literally! A little slave girl, who didn't believe in God, was known in the town for telling people's fortunes. She was possessed by a spirit that helped her tell fortunes. Her masters, who also did not know God, loved getting the money people paid her to tell their fortunes.

One day, however, the slave girl began chasing after Paul and Silas in the streets, yelling, "These men are servants of the Most High God, who are telling you the way to be saved." Now that was true. But she didn't believe it. It was just something the spirit made her say.

For days, the girl shouted after Paul and Silas as they traveled the streets of Corinth. Finally, Paul grew weary of it. He also felt very sorry for the poor girl. So he said to the spirit, "In the name of Jesus Christ, I command you to come out of her!"

And right then the spirit did.

After that, the slave girl couldn't tell fortunes anymore. She was still a slave, but she was able to hear and understand God's Word. Then she could have a new life in Him!

A Verse to Remember

Teach me your way, O Lord;
lead me in a straight path.

— Psalm 27:11

What About You?

God is leading you, too. Every single day. He doesn't force you to do right, but He helps you do right. That's why praying helps you decide what to do when you have a problem. Praying brings you closer to God. Being close to God is the best place in the world to be when you're trying to figure out something. Because no matter what your problem is, God already knows the answer to it!

What are some problems you are facing today? Write them here:

_____

_____

Ric Finds the Lord

Help Ric find his way through the confusing maze of the world's ideas to a true faith in God. The solution is on page 190.

Signs of the Times Puzzle

Add the Secret Letter "L" for "led by the Lord" to space 14 of the puzzle.

Chapter 3

What About Me?

Brittany could hardly wait for her parents to get home from their marriage enrichment weekend. She was so excited! She wanted to tell them everything that happened: playing with the babies, the birthday party in the park, romping with Sweetie and Hope, Ric's move to Summer City.

Besides, if the Christian weekend for couples went as well as Brittany hoped, her parents would come home bubbling over with love for each other. And for her. *Oh, that would be wonderful*, she thought. Especially after all the fighting they used to do.

Before the Zone 56 party that Sunday night, Brittany had planned a big welcome for her parents. First, she smoothed a fancy tablecloth across the dining room table and set two tall candlesticks in the center. Then she carefully arranged three place settings of her mother's best china on the covered table. After that she made sure there was still a pan of lasagna in the freezer that she could use for the main course. Then she prepared a tossed salad and put it in the fridge, and set a few cans of veggies on the counter, ready to heat. Not a four-star restaurant maybe, but close enough! She wanted her parents to know how much she loved them.

As Brittany left the church and walked toward her house, she almost shivered with anticipation. Had her parents beat her home?

No, there was no car in the driveway. No light in the living room. And the front door was still locked. *Good*, she thought. *That gives me time to finish cooking everything before they get here.*

Hope and Sweetie met her at the door, tails wagging madly at her return. She hugged them, then rushed into the kitchen to heat the oven for the lasagna. As the smells of hot food started to fill the house, Hope and Sweetie began whining for their own dinner. So Brittany quickly fed them their dinner, then finished heating the beans and corn, and pulled the cooked lasagna from the oven.

Everything was ready! Brittany brought out the salad plates. She opened the sparkling cider she'd been cooling in the fridge, ready to pour into her mom's fancy crystal goblets. Then she glanced at the clock. *Almost eight – surely they'll be here any time now,* she thought.

8:00 passed, then 8:30…and 8:45…and 9:00.

Brittany was getting nervous. She anxiously called the church to find someone with whom to share her concern, but everyone had left already. Then, as much as she hated to bother him, she called Pastor McConahan at home.

"Now, sweetie, don't worry," he said. "I have that retreat schedule right in front of me. It was over at 6:00. Then it would take them about an hour or two to pack up and drive back to Circleville. Maybe they stopped somewhere on the way. Would you like someone to come over and wait with you?"

"No, thank you," she said and hung up the phone. *The retreat was over at 6:00? That was over three hours ago!* she calculated. *Where in the world were they?*

By the time she called Miss Kotter, it was 9:30. Her once steaming hot dinner was now stone cold. And Brittany was crying.

"Should I call the police, Miss Kotter?" she asked her Sunday school teacher. "I'm scared. What if they were in an accident? I don't know what to do!"

"I'll be right over, Brit," Miss Kotter said.

Miss Kotter arrived with a warm hug for Brittany. Then she suggested they bow for prayer, asking God to protect Brittany's parents and soothe Brittany's fears. After the prayer, Brittany felt better. Sort of.

Her parents finally showed up at 10:00. "I fixed dinner for you!" Brittany said, angry and pouting. "Now everything's ruined. I was so worried about you!"

"Oh, Brittany!" her mother cried. "We thought you were still at Jenna's house. Your dad and I took the long way home so we could swing by the park at Crystal River where your dad proposed. We thought that would be a good place to pray and ask God to help us start our marriage over the right way.

"We decided we're going to make some changes around here, too," added her father. "Your mother's going to take a couple months off work so we can all have more time together."

Miss Kotter smiled. "I'd better get going so you can get started on that family time," she said. As she hugged Brittany good-bye, she whispered, "Slice the lasagna and put it in the microwave for a minute or two. It'll be better than ever!"

It was. With a full tummy and a happy heart, Brittany went to bed that night blissfully happy.

That's how she woke up the next morning, too. At least until breakfast. She was so glad to have her parents back...but they weren't looking at her. If they weren't holding hands they were patting each other's arms, or gazing into each other's eyes. She even caught her mom sitting on her dad's lap! *It's like they're dating again*, Brittany thought grumpily.

She felt like a fifth wheel, like a speck on the ceiling, completely left out — as if she didn't even belong there!

Finally, she had had enough. "Ex-cuuuse me!" Brittany huffed and ran to her room. She fell sobbing on her bed.

Her mother rushed after her. "Brittany, honey!" she cried. "We didn't mean to exclude you. It's just that your father and I have so much catching up to do as a couple, and as a family."

Brittany sat up and wiped her eyes.

"In fact, that's one reason I'm going to take some time off from work," her mom explained. "We need a family vacation. All three of us together. How does going to Florida sound to you? We can spend some time with your Grandma and Grandpa Wilson, and maybe even go to a few amusement parks."

"Oh, Mom!" Brittany cried.

And the two of them hugged each other so hard that all the hurt and jealousy popped right out of Brittany's heart and disappeared into thin air. For good.

· PTS ·

· Good News · from God's Word

Did you ever get jealous of one of your brothers or sisters? Maybe you thought your sister was prettier or more graceful than you. Or your brother seemed to get all A's without even cracking a book. You might have thought your parents favored them, and it just didn't seem fair. Here's a Bible story about a girl who seemed left out of things for a while.

Zeruiah Is Glad for Her Life

FROM 1 CHRONICLES 2:13-17

David came from a big family. He was the youngest of seven boys. There were also two girls, Zeruiah and her sister, Abigail.

Everyone thought the oldest boy of the family was the most important. He was tall and handsome. They thought David was the least important. When the prophet Samuel came to visit their family, they didn't even bother inviting David in from the fields to meet him.

They probably thought the two girls were even less important. But Zeruiah and Abigail worked hard.

They grew up, got married and had children. Zeruiah had three little boys. Her life was quiet.

Meanwhile, her little brother David became one of the most famous men in the land. First, he was known as a musician to King Saul. Then he killed the giant Goliath with a slingshot. Finally, he was made king himself.

Zeruiah probably thought her life was very ordinary compared to David's. It would have been very easy for her to be jealous of her brother.

But instead, Zeruiah focused on raising her boys to love God. They grew up to be remarkable young men. One became a great runner. Today he'd probably be in the Olympics! Another, Joab, became King David's general. The third turned out to be one of David's mighty men.

Zeruiah knew God wanted her to be a good mother. Even though her calling was not perhaps as glamorous as her brother's, she obeyed God. The result was three men who could continue God's work.

A Verse to Remember

*How good and pleasant it is when
brothers live together in unity!*

— **Psalm 133:1**

What About You?

Right now is a good time to realize that you will never be exactly like someone else. Someone else's eyes will always be bluer or greener or blacker or browner. Someone else will always be taller or shorter or thinner or plumper. Quit comparing yourself to them! Compare yourself to yourself — and to the wonderful young woman God is helping you to be. Be excited about your future. God is!

What are some of your best qualities? Write them here:

_____

_____

Dinner by Candlelight

Maybe you would like to prepare a special dinner for your own parents or family for a birthday, anniversary or other celebration. Or even for a "just because" event! Here are some things to consider as you plan:

❤ Set a date. Are there other family activities that might conflict with your event?

❤ Time of day. Will you serve breakfast, lunch, dinner, dessert or a snack?

❤ Decide where to serve. Would your meal be best eaten in the kitchen, the dining room, outside on the patio or in another location?

❤ Write out your meal plan. What is something you and your family like to eat that is not too difficult to prepare? Don't plan for too much extravagance — a few things done well is always a better strategy.

❤ Write a shopping list. Are the items you need affordable and easily available? How will you get to the grocery store and pay for your items? It is faster and easier to use canned, packaged, frozen or other partially-prepared food. You can also buy complete meals from a deli or restaurant.

❤ Give yourself plenty of cooking time. If you decide to cook from scratch, be sure you use a good cookbook and follow it faithfully. Be aware of how long each food takes to prepare. If the frozen meat takes an hour to thaw, add that to your preparation time.

❤ Safety first! If you use the stove have an adult nearby in case of an emergency. Watch out for boiling water, steam, hot oil and hot surfaces like the oven door and burners. Make sure the gas burners, if you have them, actually have flames when you turn them on.

♥ Cooking also means cleaning. Be smart and clean up as you work.

♥ Set the table. While the food is cooking, arrange the place settings. Try stuffing the napkins in the glasses and fanning out the tops. Even paper napkins in paper cups look fancier that way!

♥ Figure out how you will serve the food. You could set up a self-serve buffet on a side table or counter, spoon the food onto the plates before you distribute them or simply place the food on the table in platters and bowls "family-style."

♥ Encourage prayer before you eat. Ask your family to hold hands and thank God for the food and for each family member.

♥ Eat and enjoy! As you clean up afterward, put all of the leftover food in the refrigerator. Leftovers by candlelight are tasty, too!

Signs of the Times Puzzle

Add Secret Letter "N" for "not jealous" to space 10 of the puzzle.

Chapter 4

The Whole Truth and...

Brittany was desperate to tell someone about her family's plans! But when she called Sam's house, she discovered that Sam had already left for her sewing class.

Sam rode her bike to the design studio, but she might as well have flown through the air. She was so excited! She had with her a notebook, some fabric scraps she liked and the fashion designs she'd been working on. She wished she'd heard from the fashion design contest that she'd entered in the spring. It sure would be fun to pull out a blue ribbon and tell the teacher, "Oh, by the way, this is a little something you might be interested in."

But Sam did have something else special with her: color copies of some of her Grandma Pearson's work. Just in case her teacher was interested!

Walking into Miss Garry's room at the design studio was like walking into a whole new world. It was alive with brilliant fabrics, color photographs, portable sewing machines, art tables and a few computers. In addition to Sam, 15 other girls and young women were there. Plus three guys! *That's funny*, Sam thought. *I never even considered that guys might be here. But I guess men are some of the most talented fashion designers in the world!*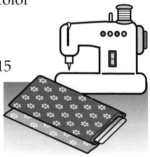

Miss Garry was as young and striking as a fashion model. She was tall and thin. Her hair was swept into a French knot. She even had a New York accent. But her smile was warm and down-to-earth.

"Good morning, students," she began. "We have a lot of techniques and skills to cover this summer. Of course, you don't have to sew well to design well. But you can't hope to design well if you don't know something about the properties of different kinds of cloth; how clothes are constructed to fit human bodies, especially women's; and how the hang of garments is affected by cutting with or against the bias, by lining and stiffening, kinds of stitching and so on. I'll be introducing you to all kinds of sewing, and how to use computers in fashion design. Some people call it the 'rag trade.' "

Sam smiled at Miss Garry. She was already liking what she heard!

"But before you are introduced to all of that," Miss Garry said as she turned to a student on the first row, "we want to be introduced to all of you. Please tell us your name, where you're from, and why you signed up for this class. Also, if you brought with you any drawings or clothes you've actually designed and sewn, please share those with us, too."

All of the students had brought something to show. Sam could hardly wait to pull out her own work. Finally, it was her turn.

"I'm Sam Pearson. I go to Madison Middle School," she began. "I've always wanted to design clothes. I used to draw clothes for my paper dolls. And my mom helped me make clothes for my dolls. But I didn't think I could ever be good enough to do it for real.

"Then my Grandma Pearson came to visit me. She said she entered a design contest when she was young and won it. Then she went on to New York to be a real designer. She encouraged me to enter a contest myself. But I don't know how I did yet. Anyway, I heard about this class, and I'm so excited to be here!"

Miss Garry nodded. "Wonderful, Sam. We're

glad to have you with us. Want to show us what you brought?"

Sam pulled everything out of her stuffed backpack — drawings, notebook and all. Even Grandma Pearson's sketches! "Here's a wedding gown I designed. And some pajamas, and a sweater. And a special outfit for skating."

Miss Garry nodded politely as Sam held up her drawings. Then suddenly she walked up to Sam's desk. "Sam, you are much too modest. Class, look at these pictures! Why, I can hardly believe how good the work is! Congratulations!"

Sam's heart fell down into her shoes. Miss Garry had stopped looking at Sam's work. The designs she was praising were Grandma Pearson's!

Excited, the teacher held up one of Sam's grandmother's sketches. "Now, class, this is retro," she explained, "derived from a style popular long before Sam was even born. Retro is in. Very chic!"

"Well, I, uh…" Sam knew that "retro" meant repeating old stuff. Grandma hadn't repeated anything old. Those fashions were actually in style when she drew them!

"And excellent watercolor work. All right, class, I see we have a lot of talent with us. I'm looking forward to a wonderful summer session. Now, if you're ready to take notes, I'll explain some of our class procedures."

Sam's hands wrote down her teacher's words, but her mind was whirling out in space. She hadn't meant to deceive her teacher. What in the world should she do now?

"It's not your fault," a tiny voice in one side of her head seemed to say. "She didn't give you a chance to explain."

"But you could have anyway," a voice in the other side of Sam's head argued. "Go ahead, put your hand up and tell her."

"Don't be stupid," demanded the first voice. "You'd only embarrass her. Come on, don't make such a big deal of it. It's just a little white lie."

"God's children don't tell lies of any kind," said the other voice. "God is the God of Truth. You go right up there after class and explain. It's the only right thing to do."

Sam felt like running out of the room right then and letting those voices argue to each other. But she knew the good voice of her conscience was right, and not the bad voice of temptation.

After class, she waited to see Miss Garry alone and explain the whole situation.

"Thank you for telling me, Sam," Miss Garry said with another one of her warm smiles. Sam knew immediately that she had done the right thing by clearing up the misunderstanding. "You know, if your grandmother learned to do that well, I'm sure you soon will, too. Meanwhile, do you mind if I display your grandma's drawings in our classroom? I think they will inspire us all."

Mind? Nothing could have thrilled Sam more!

· Good News · from God's Word

This is a sad Bible story about a woman who knew the truth, yet chose not to tell it.

Sapphira Chooses Lies
FROM ACTS 5:1-11

The new Christians were so excited! They saw Jesus die, which was horribly sad, but then they saw Him alive again. He rose right through the clouds up to heaven. They had been filled with God's Holy Spirit. So Peter and the others began telling everyone about Jesus.

The disciples healed the sick in Jesus' name. They spoke before mighty rulers. Some disciples were punished for preaching about Jesus, but they kept on doing it anyway. All of Jerusalem was amazed.

Some people were so touched by all this that they wanted to show their love by sharing. There were many poor widows and orphans who needed help, and others who couldn't get jobs because they were now Christians.

So all of the wealthier believers began bringing their extra money, food and other supplies to the church leaders to make sure no one went hungry. All of the poor or jobless believers appreciated these good people.

"Let's sell some of our land and give the money to the church, too," Ananias, one of the new Christians, said to his wife Sapphira.

"Yes, let's do it," she agreed.

So they sold their property for a large sum of money. "Now we can give it all to the church..." Ananias said, "or we can pretend to give it all but really keep some for ourselves."

"What a great idea!" Sapphira selfishly decided. "That way everyone will think we're really wonderful and we can still buy whatever we want."

God didn't tell them they had to sell that land. They chose to sell it. Then when they did sell it, God didn't tell them they had to give it all to the church. He didn't even tell them they had to give any of it away. What He does tell us — and has always told people — is that we must not lie. God is the God of all Truth. Satan is the father of all lies.

Ananias came to the church. "I sold my property and now I'm giving all my money to God!" he declared. But it was a lie. God immediately struck him dead!

Then Sapphira lied about the money, too. She also fell down dead!

That was a terrible punishment. But God says lies are very serious sins. They hurt people. They hurt businesses. They can even cost innocent people their lives. God says He hates lies. We should, too! Think twice before you lie.

A Verse to Remember

A truthful witness gives honest testimony,
but a false witness tells lies.

— Proverbs 12:17

Wipe-Out

Have you ever told lies? Were you or are you ashamed of them? Write them on some facial tissue or toilet paper. Then pray and ask God to forgive you for telling those lies — and flush them right down the toilet. That's how completely God has promised to forgive you. Then pray and ask God to help you avoid the temptation to lie the next time.

I lied to my Mom.

Right Side, Wrong Side

In each of these situations, which one of the "voices" should you follow? Circle your answers.

1. At the mall, you see a $20 bill on the floor by a cash register. But no one else sees it.

continued on next page…

a. "Go ahead, slip it in your wallet and keep it to yourself. After all, finders keepers!"

b. "Pick it up and show it to the sales clerk, explaining where you found it."

2. Your last name is the same as a famous person about whom you are supposed to do a report.

a. "Pretend that you're related. Maybe you'll get extra points that way!"

b. "No way! Do your research and do it right."

3. While at a neighbor's home, you knock over a vase and break it. No one saw you.

a. "Quick! Say you have to go home right away, and don't let on that anything is wrong."

b. "'Fess up, help clean up the mess, and ask if you can pay for it. If it's too expensive, maybe you can pay a little each week on it. Or talk with your parents about replacing it with a new one."

4. You answer the phone. Your sister's boyfriend thinks you're her.

a. "Tell him you're flattered, but..."

b. "Hey, it's not your fault he's so dumb. Keep stringing him along until he catches on."

5. Your pastor keeps telling people you're a "fine Christian girl." But you've never really made a decision for Christ.

continued on next page...

a. "Why bother if everyone's already fooled? You're the only one who knows the truth deep inside."

b. "God knows the truth, and He's the one who counts. Why not make your decision for Christ today, and turn that 'lie' into truth!"

The answers are on page 190.

Signs of the Times Puzzle

Add the Secret Letter "T" for "truth-telling" to space 16 of the puzzle.

Chapter 5

Mowing and Meowing

For LaToya's first day of volunteer "yard duty" at Mrs. Greenleaf's, her PTs decided to give her a helping hand. Even Kevin, Josh and Tyler from Zone 56 showed up. No one had really tackled her yard since the clean-up day last fall. And Mrs. Greenleaf, who was nearly blind and in a wheelchair, and her roommate Mrs. Ryan, who was also frail, couldn't do much on their own.

"We had everyone here that day!" Maria recounted to Brittany, the newest PT, about their fall clean-up. "Even Mr. Talley. You should have seen this place before we started working on it!"

Brittany wrinkled her nose. "No, thank you. It's bad enough now."

The fruit trees were thriving, thanks to the great pruning job the volunteers had done last fall. Mrs. Greenleaf's roses were in full bloom, along with the gladiolas — and, unfortunately, a jungle of weeds. Plus plenty of aphids, snails, and…

"Yuck!" Brittany cried. "Help! I've got ants all over me."

LaToya grabbed the hose and squirted Brittany with it. Soon they were all in a water fight! After a few minutes they were cooled down and ready to work again. The girls pulled and cut and trimmed. The boys ran the  Pearsons' lawn mower and clipped the hedge. They even planted hollyhock and sunflower seeds by the front porch. It was hot work on a hot day.

Meanwhile, Mrs. Greenleaf and Mrs. Ryan sat on the front porch, handing out lemonade and homemade peanut butter cookies as the workers took frequent cool-down breaks. As they glided in their porch swing, the two elderly ladies encouraged the kids along.

"Oh, my!" they exclaimed. "This is wonderful!"

"We just love you dear, sweet, young people!"

"Have another cookie. Here, have two."

During one break, Brittany wiped the sweat off her forehead and gulped some bottled water. "Could you guys please help me keep an eye on the time?" she asked her PTs. "I've got to get home by noon because I promised my mom I would help pack for our trip to Florida."

"When do you leave on your vacation?" asked LaToya.

"Right after church tomorrow," Brittany replied. "I can hardly wait! I've never been to Florida before. But I hate bailing out on you guys while you're still working here."

"That's OK. The rest of us have to stop working at noon too, Brit," LaToya said. "My family's going to a Juneteenth festival in Summer City later so I have to get home, too."

Sara tied up a bag full of lawn clippings. "A June what?"

"It's a holiday called Juneteenth and it's especially for African-Americans. See, when the Civil War ended in April of 1865, all the slaves were freed. But people didn't have radio or TV then, so the news didn't reach Texas 'til June 19th that summer. From that day on, former slaves celebrated on that day. But 'June 19th' seemed like a long title, so people shortened it to "Juneteenth" and that's what it's still called today."

Sara grabbed another bag to fill. "Wow, I didn't know that, LaToya. I hope you have all have a great time."

"What are you doing for Father's Day tomorrow?" Sam asked the group as she readjusted her now-limp ponytail. "My mom wanted to take my dad to a fancy restaurant. But he said he'd rather put on jeans and an old shirt and go fishing at Lucky Lake. So that's what we're going to do!"

Maria looked at Sam. "Oh, wow, my dad loves fishing! I didn't even think of something like that. But Mom is planning a nice dinner for him at home. Then again, maybe we could just pack up the dinner and take it with us to the lake. I'll check with Mom." Sonya wheeled up with another trash bag.

"Ooooo…my dad and I love fishing, too. Maybe we could get all of our families to go. I heard the ranger just restocked the lake to make up for some of the fish lost in the flood last spring."

"Sounds like a great idea," Sara agreed.

By noon, everything was mown, trimmed, raked and watered.

"See you in two weeks," LaToya said wearily to Mrs. Greenleaf.

"Thank you, thank you. Everything looks just beautiful!" sighed Mrs. Greenleaf. And she meant it, too. Even though she was almost blind and couldn't see the actual work the group had done, Mrs. Greenleaf felt the love and care with which they did it.

Just then everyone heard faintly, "Meow!" It was coming from under Mrs. Greenleaf"s porch.

"Kittens!" Jenna cried. "Did you hear that? Mrs. Greenleaf, you have kittens!"

The elderly woman frowned. "Do not! Impossible! Used to have a dog. Never had a cat, though. Can't stand them. Slinking around in the dark and all that. Making all that noise. Nope, never had a cat."

Kevin peered under the front porch. "Well, you have one now, Mrs. Greenleaf. She's away from her babies right now. But you're also the proud owner of one…two…three…four…five…six little kittens!"

"Six!" squealed the girls at once. "What do they look like?"

"It's kind of hard to tell in the dark. But I see spots and stripes and all kinds of colors. They look like they were probably just born."

Mrs. Greenleaf looked troubled. "But I can't have cats. I don't like cats. Never did. Oh, dear! What will I do with all of them?"

"Don't you worry," Sam said as she patted Mrs. Greenleaf's shriveled hands. "My mom works at an animal shelter. We'll make sure your cat family has plenty of food and water until the kittens are old enough to take them all to the shelter. Meanwhile, we'll take turns setting out food and water. Right, guys?"

"Yeah!" the others agreed.

Yet old Mrs. Greenleaf just stared into space. "But I don't like cats," she kept repeating to Mrs. Ryan. "I'd never hurt them, of course. I mean, not in a million years. But I just don't like them. Never did."

Josh gave her a hug. "Well, Mrs. Greenleaf. Guess what? Maybe they like you!"

· Good News · from God's Word

The Zone 56 members were glad to help out two elderly friends. Here's a Bible story about another woman who needed help.

A Grieving Mother Asks for Help

FROM MARK 7:24-30

Jesus often traveled around telling people about God. One time He left Israel to go all the way to Tyre. This large city was on the Mediterranean Sea coast in Phoenicia, which is now the country of Lebanon. Most of the people who lived there were not believers.

Jesus was invited to someone's home there. "Don't tell anyone else I'm here," He said. He needed a rest. Also, many of the non-believing rulers wanted to hurt Him.

But it was impossible to keep a wonderful secret like that! Even people that far away knew about Jesus. So instead of resting, He preached, He taught and He healed the sick. He could do anything!

When one Gentile woman heard that Jesus was right there in her city, she was thrilled because she had a very sick little girl. "I must see Jesus!" she decided. "No one else can heal my little girl. But I know He can!"

So, leaving her little girl home sick in bed, she ran to see Jesus.

She fell at His feet. "Oh, please!" she begged. "Heal my little girl!"

Then Jesus said something strange. "It's not right to take children's bread and throw it to dogs," He said. He wasn't being mean. He meant that God wanted Him to tell the Gospel to the Jews first before reaching out to other people.

"Yes, Lord!" she replied. "But, oh, even puppies under the table get to eat the children's crumbs." Just like today, dogs in Bible times liked to beg at meals.

When Jesus heard her call Him "Lord," He was very touched. That meant that she really believed in Him as her Savior, the Son of God.

"What great faith!" He said. "Go, your daughter is healed."

The woman thanked Him and rushed home.

Her little daughter was indeed well. The woman's faith had saved her daughter's life.

A Verse to Remember

*Look after orphans and widows
in their distress.*

— *James 1:27*

What About You?

People who need your help are all around you, even if you don't see them. Maybe your mom needs a hand in the kitchen. Your sister might be glad for you to help her do her hair a new way. Or maybe your brother would like for you to pitch some softballs to him so he can practice batting. A new mother you know might be thrilled for help with babysitting. A young children's Sunday school class teacher might like a hand with crafts or snack time.

Where can you help someone this week? Write your ideas here:

_____

_____

You also need help from others — your teacher, pastor, doctor, coach, parents and neighbors.

God intends for us to help one another, so don't be too proud to ask for help. On the other hand, don't expect them to do your work for you.

Peanutty-Perfect Cookies

Here's how to make the peanut butter cookies that Mrs. Greenleaf and Mrs. Ryan served their helpers.

What You Need

- non-stick cooking spray
- 12 tablespoons unsalted butter, softened
- 1 cup sugar
- 1¼ cups peanut butter
- 1 egg
- ½ teaspoon vanilla extract
- 1½ cups all-purpose flour
- ½ teaspoon baking soda

What to Do

1. Preheat the oven to 350°.

2. Spray baking sheets with non-stick spray.

3. In the mixing bowl, cream the butter with the sugar.

4. Beat in the peanut butter, egg and vanilla. Mix well.

5. Sift together the flour and baking soda. Add it to the cookie dough and mix well.

6. Drop the batter by tablespoonfuls onto the baking sheets, leaving 2 inches between the cookies.

7. Dip a fork in some extra sugar. Gently flatten each

continued on next page…

cookie with the fork, then do it again the opposite direction so you get a cross-hatch look.

8. Bake the cookies for 10 minutes or until they are lightly browned and firm.

9. Remove the cookies from the oven and allow them to cool on the sheets for a few minutes.

10. Lift each cookie from the sheet and move it to a wire cooling rack. Brown paper grocery bags, torn open and laid flat, also make a good cooling place.

Note: Some people are allergic to peanuts so tell people your cookies have peanuts in them before you serve them.

Signs of the Times Puzzle

Add the Secret Letter "S" for "serving others" to space 3 of the puzzle.

Chapter 6

Gone Fishin'

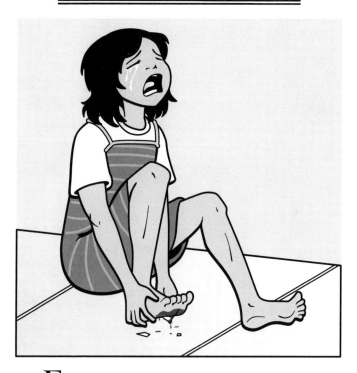

Everyone agreed that spending Father's Day afternoon at Lucky Lake was a great idea. The dads, kids and some of the moms loved fishing. It was like one big, happy family!

Miss Kotter also dropped by — and caught the most fish of all! After that, everyone called her "Miss Fisher" the rest of the day. Laughing, she admitted that she actually hated the taste of fish, so she "donated" her entire catch to Granny B., who eagerly wrapped them up to fry later.

The PTs looked for wildflowers, chased butterflies and rowed out on the lake. Even Suzie, who had fallen in the lake last fall at Sam's birthday party, behaved this time. Sara's mom suggested that everyone choose a buddy for safety. Tina, LaToya's sister who was a nursing student, also made sure everyone knew she had a stocked first aid kit with her in case anyone did get hurt.

Later, everyone gathered for a potluck picnic. The PTs quickly filled their plates and grabbed a table together.

"I'm sure glad Sara thought of this," Maria said as she squeezed mustard on her hot dog.

"Are you kidding?" Sam protested. "Sara didn't think of it. I did. Don't you remember?"

"Well, that's not the way I remember it," Maria replied. "At least Sara thought to ask Tina to bring the first aid kit."

"Wait a minute!" Jenna interrupted. "What are you talking about? That was my idea."

Maria frowned. "Well, exc-u-u-se me. And I suppose the recipe for Mama's enchiladas, which you all gobbled down without so much as a thank you, was one of your ideas, too. Right?" And she stormed off.

The other girls stared after her. "Oh, who needs her?" LaToya snapped.

Hurtful words and bad feelings had ruined their fun, just the way last spring's flood had trashed the park around them. As beautiful as the lake still was, the grounds were a mess. A mess that wasn't going away by itself.

"My family tried to clean it up," sighed the  park ranger, who stopped by to greet everyone. "But there's just too much of it. I could sure use some volunteers."

"Maybe our Midland and Circleville churches could help," Jenna's brother, Tony, suggested.

Jenna's dad nodded. "And Scouts and other clubs. But it usually takes weeks or months to pull off something like that."

Just then, Maria's little sister, Lolita, let out a wail of pain. Mr. Moreno rushed to her side and held her foot to inspect it. Blood gushed everywhere.

"This is a really bad cut!" cried Mr. Moreno. "It looks like there's some broken glass stuck in there. We need to get her to a hospital!"

Tina grabbed the first aid kit and tried to stop the bleeding. "Let's go to Midland General, where I work," she said. "It's closest, and I know everyone there."

Mr. Maxwell, the park ranger, was alarmed. "This is just what I was afraid of with all that trash lying around!" he cried as he reached in his pocket for his keys. "My SUV is closest. I'll drive you to the hospital."

Tina wrapped Lolita's foot as best she could and Mr. Moreno lifted Lolita up into Mr. Maxwell's waiting vehicle. Then Mr. and Mrs. Moreno climbed in on either side of Lolita and Tina jumped in the front passenger seat.

After they sped off, everyone else quietly helped clean up the leftover food and pack it away. The fun atmosphere had abruptly ended.

"I hope poor little Lolita is all right," Sonya whispered.

Le's face was just as sad. "She was bleeding so much. I'm scared for her."

"I feel bad for something else, too," Sara added. "I think we hurt Maria's feelings. And I don't know what to do about it."

Sam shook her head. "I don't, either. Maybe she'll just get over it."

Before the families left the park, they gathered in a circle and prayed for Lolita. "I think I'll stop by the hospital and see how she's doing," Miss Kotter said.

"Sonya and I will go with you," decided Mr. Silverhorse.

"Besides," Miss Kotter added, "a friend of mine is a newspaper reporter. I'll call him from the hospital and tell him how this trash can cause injuries. Maybe he'll want to do a story on it."

By the next morning, the newspaper had Lolita's picture right on the front page, along with pictures of Lucky Lake and some of the trash that had injured her. "Fortunately, little Lolita Moreno will recover," the article said. "But the next child might not be so lucky."

The story also included statements from Mr. Maxwell and the mayors of both Midland and Circleville. "Next Saturday has been declared Lucky

Lake Day," the article announced. "There will be a clean-up from 8 until noon with jobs for all ages and abilities. Wear sturdy shoes. Bring gloves and rubber boots if you have them. Trash bags and trash bins will be provided."

The PTs were thrilled that the lake would be cleaned up. "I'll be there next Saturday and hope you will, too," Miss Kotter said when she called each PT to remind them. "Jesus wants us to do good for individuals, and for our whole community."

But as everyone excitedly planned for Saturday, Sam was upset about Maria, who hadn't talked to any of the PTs all week. Sam called Sara.

"We've got to do something about this thing with Maria," she said. "I can't stand it. I miss her!"

"I know," said Sara. Then she brightened. "Hey, I know just the thing. Let's get the other PTs. We have shopping to do."

The next morning, the PTs stopped by the Morenos with two bouquets of flowers. One was for little Lolita, who was sitting in a rocking chair with her foot and leg bandaged up. The other was for her big sister.

"We're sorry we hurt your feelings," Sam said. "Please forgive us." And she handed her the bouquet.

"Oh, wow," Maria replied as she smelled the flowers. "How could I stay mad at you guys? After all, we are the PTs!"

· Good News · from God's Word

The PTs wanted to do something good for their environment. They also learned they had to do good to each other, especially when Maria's feelings were hurt. That's the same lesson these Bible women needed to learn.

Euodia and Syntyche Learn to Love

FROM PHILIPPIANS 4:2-3

The apostle Paul traveled through many countries preaching about Jesus. Some of his friends traveled with him, including Timothy, Barnabas and Luke. They helped lead many people to Christ, and they started many churches. Later, Paul wrote letters to his new Christian friends in these cities. Some of these letters became books in the New Testament.

One of the churches Paul wrote to was the church at Philippi. This was a prosperous city run by the Romans in the country of Macedonia. Many of the men there had served in the Roman army and were proud of it. Some even spoke Latin instead of Greek. Hardly anyone there was Jewish or had studied the Old Testament.

But Paul loved these new believers. And they loved Paul. When they found out he was in prison in Rome, they took up a collection and sent him money. He wrote a letter to thank them and to tell them not to worry about him. He also encouraged them to continue living for Christ and telling others about Him.

But Paul had something sad to say, too. There were two women in the church at Philippi, Euodia and Syntyche, who had done a lot of good for Paul and for everyone else. Then somehow they had a falling out with each other. The Bible doesn't tell us what happened. But the whole church knew about it and was hurt because of it. Even Paul, far away in Rome, knew about it! Maybe people were taking sides over this disagreement and saying mean things behind each other's backs.

In his letter, Paul begs these two women to make up as loving Christians should. He asks the other believers to help them in this and to bring them together and let them talk about it. Then they were to pray about it and forgive each other.

We don't know if they actually did what Paul asked. But it is still a good lesson. God wants all of us to get along, especially in the church.

A Verse to Remember

Jesus…went around doing good.

— *Acts 10:38*

What About You?

Have your feelings ever been hurt? What did you do about it? Yell? Talk about someone? Go to your room and cry? Get mad and say, "I'll show them!" If you can remember such a time, write about it here. Maybe you're still feeling hurt about it!

_____

_____

_____

The best thing to do is ask God to help you not to feel so hurt. Then forgive in your heart the person who hurt you. Maybe that person didn't mean to do it. Maybe they didn't even know they hurt you! Even if they did, ask God to help you to put it behind you. Then get on with being the wonderful daughter of God your Heavenly Father wants you to be. Ask God to help you not to be hurt so easily — and to remind you to deal lovingly with the person who hurt you.

Feelings!

We all have many kinds of feelings or emotions. That's how God made us. However, we need to make sure our emotions don't make us do wrong or hurtful things to ourselves or to others. From the column on the right, select the emotion to fill in each blank in the rhyming clues on the left.

1. When I'm sad and down, it's true,
   I tell people that I'm feeling _____.

2. Sometimes, just like a joyful song,
   I'm feeling _____ all day long.

3. When meeting a new girl or guy,
   Sometimes I'm suddenly quite _____.

4. This or that? What should I do?
   I often get _____, don't you?

5. I try to hold my temper in
   When I'm _____, so I don't sin.

6. I wish I had great clothes like Marie.
   But _____ I should never, ever be.

7. When I've done something good, I think
   Life's really great. I'm _____ pink.

8. I want to find a place to hide
   When I'm _____ and terrified.

9. I've been asked to sing a song.
   I'm _____. Will I sing it wrong?

10. I got four As and just one B.
    My mother is so _____ of me!

a. angry
b. jealous
c. afraid
d. proud
e. blue
f. upbeat
g. confused
h. shy
i. tickled
j. nervous

The answers are on page 190.

Signs of the Times Puzzle

Add the Secret Letter "D" for "doing good" to space 20 of the puzzle.

Chapter 7

Summertime and...Yeah, Right!

LaToya pushed the lawnmower into the garage. "If I hear someone sing that song about 'summertime and the living is easy' one more time, I'll scream!" she grumbled as she marched into the house.

Granny B. had just wheeled in from her garden.

"Oh, LaToya, wait 'til you see my fine tomatoes!" she said. "We'll have a bumper crop next month. And we should have plenty of corn on the cob for July 4th. Want to come out and see?"

LaToya grabbed a cold drink from the refrigerator and collapsed on the sofa. "Later, Granny B. I don't feel like it right now. I just got back from doing Mrs. Greenleaf's lawn and feeding her cat. We're all taking turns with cat duty, you know."

"And how are those kittens?"

"Cute as can be. One's gold, one's all black, one's calico spotted, one's all white and two are gray-striped. Their eyes are just starting to open. The mommy cat looks sort of like a Siamese. She must be wild, though. She hisses every time I'm around. But when I start to leave, she rushes out and eats like she's starving."

"She probably is, the poor dear. Hope they find a good home for her. Wouldn't mind having a kitty around the house, myself."

Then she added, "We'd best get ready. Pastor McConahan said he'd be by at noon to pick us up for Whispering Pines. It's so much fun to read letters to the residents there and help Pastor with his Bible study. You know, I think they look at me in my wheelchair and it helps them not feel so bad about being in wheelchairs themselves."

Volunteering with Granny B. at the nursing home, attending gymnastics class, practicing her guitar and mowing two lawns, LaToya was tired already. And summer had barely begun.

The other PTs were just as busy. Jenna and

Maria had tennis classes every day at Shawnee Park. Both were doing well at it, especially Maria. "You've really got power in your serve, girl," Jenna complimented her.

"But I can't leap as high as you do for rebounds," Maria replied. "You know, if we keep this up, maybe we can play for the girls' tennis team when we get to high school. That is, if the school even has a girls' team."

Jenna laughed. "Well, if they don't, we'll just start one!"

Besides tennis, Jenna helped babysit her three younger sisters and took ballet lessons. Maria helped her mom with a big housecleaning job and with her garden. Le took violin and computer lessons.

Both Le and Maria were also taking a short teacher-training class at Midland's Grace Church to prepare them to be helpers at the church's VBS right after July 4th. Pastor Andy gave them rides over to Midland each time and Shannon Hendricks' mom gave them rides back home. Shannon was the friend from Midland they met at Winter Camp.

Sam babysat Petie and Suzie part-time. She continued going to her design class and spent a lot of time on homework for the class. She never knew sewing would be so hard! Fortunately, Le and her mom were excellent seamstresses, so she frequently called them for advice. Each day, she opened the mailbox expectantly, hoping to find a letter from the design contest she had entered in the spring.

Sonya, who had also entered the contest, hadn't heard back, either. But she was too busy practicing for the wheelchair basketball tournament to worry about it. Wheelchair basketball was a whole new world for Sonya — a real, active sport instead of just board games! She found out that there were many skills involved in the game, such as being able to turn quickly without tipping her chair. Her arms started to show very defined muscles!

"I miss Ric," she confided to Sara with a twinkle in her eye. "He was so good at tipping me over in the snow, but now I could probably fight him off!" She laughed. "Wish he could see me now. But he has promised to watch me play in the big game."

Sara helped Miss Kotter at the rescue mission and practiced ice skating down at the rink. An indoor one, of course. The summer temperatures in Circleville were starting to get close to 100°. Sara was also looking forward to Brittany returning from vacation so they could start working on some new fall cheerleading routines.

With so much going on, the PTs almost forgot something. Something important. Something very, very important that would be there before they knew it.

Camp Porcupine!

"How are we going to raise the money to go?" Sam asked during the Lucky Lake clean-up that Saturday. She held out a large, orange trash bag for Sara to dump trash into. And what yucky trash it was! Old cans, bottles, pieces of tires, plastic bags, diapers, corn cobs — even a rusty bird cage. "Oops! I sure hope that poor bird got out first!" Sara exclaimed.

"But camp's a whole month away," Maria said. "We have plenty of time." But when she thought about how busy they all were, she reconsidered. "No, I guess we don't," she corrected herself. "OK, everyone, put your thinking caps on. How can we raise some money? And, most importantly, how can we raise it in time?"

Sara sighed. "Yeah, we need to think of something. We can plan all we want to have a great time there, but we can just kiss those plans good-bye if we don't get there at all!"

· Good News · from God's Word

The PTs had planned well for a busy summer. Now they needed to plan for camp. The Bible is full of stories of when God helped people plan for things. He has plans for us as well. Here's a Bible story that shows how God works out His plans for our good.

Queen Candace Learns of God's Plans
FROM ACTS 8:26-40

Ethiopia is a very old African nation. Based in the high mountains south of Egypt, its empire often reached out for hundreds of miles. Indeed, for a long time Ethiopia ruled over Egypt.

Apparently, this empire also reached across Africa into Sheba, a great country in the Arabian peninsula. Remember the Queen of Sheba? Some historians call her the Queen of both Ethiopia and Sheba. She's the one who came to see King Solomon and learn more about God. After that, many Ethiopians believed in God, too.

A thousand years later, one of the top Ethiopian leaders, the treasurer, went hundreds of miles away to Jerusalem to worship. As an important man from a great country, and the personal representative of Queen Candace, he traveled in one of her royal chariots. He probably took along offerings not just from him but from his queen and all the country's people.

On his way home, the treasurer began to read the Bible aloud as he rode along. But he didn't really understand it. When he read Isaiah 53:7-8, he wondered who the "he" was in the Scripture: him or someone else?

At the same time in Samaria, God's servant Philip was busy preaching in great crowds. Many people believed in God and rejoiced.

Then God said to Philip, "Leave this place and start walking down the desert road." Now that seemed strange. Why didn't God want him to stay and preach to more people where he was?

But Philip obeyed God. He started walking. And guess what he came upon on that road? Queen Candace's royal chariot. With the treasurer inside.

"Go talk to him," God told Philip. People usually didn't walk right up to royal treasurers without being asked! But Philip did as he was told. "Do you understand what you're reading?" he asked the treasurer.

"Not really," replied the treasurer. "Can you ride along with me and explain it?"

So Philip told him about God's Son, Jesus, who came to earth, died and rose from the dead. The treasurer soon believed in Jesus. He became so happy about it that as soon as they came to a stream he asked Philip to baptize him. Then Philip left the treasurer, who continued home to Ethiopia, rejoicing all the way. When he arrived there, he shared the Good News about Jesus with Queen Candace and many others.

A Verse to Remember

A man's steps are directed by the Lord.

— *Proverbs 20:24*

What About You?

Life doesn't just happen. God guides and directs our steps, but we have to do the walking ourselves. We're not robots. We're not characters in an interactive video game. We're not TV screens that God turns on and off with a remote. We are His beloved children, not His playthings.

It's not too soon in life for you to start thinking about your plans for your life, and to pray that God will show you what to do and how to do it. Right now, write down what you think God wants you to be or do when you are an adult:

_____

_____

_____

Today's date: _____

Then keep praying about it. Let God direct your steps.

Scat, Cat!

Mama Cat's six little kittens have scampered away. Help her find them and bring all six back home (turn the page sideways). The solution is on page 190.

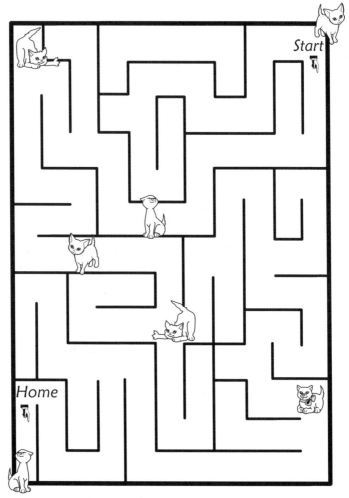

Signs of the Times Puzzle

Add the Secret Letter "O" for "open to God's plans" to space 12 of the puzzle.

Chapter 8

Red, White and Really Blue!

The Lucky Lake clean-up was a success. Crowds of volunteers filled truck after truck with trash. Besides, it was a gorgeous day. Hot and humid, but gorgeous.

The volunteers were invited to march in the

Circleville Fourth of July parade, along with the high school and middle school bands. Because school was out for the summer, the bands were made up of the previous school year's members. So Ric got to march with his saxophone along with Kevin and his other Madison Middle School buddies. Sara marched as a cheerleader. Brittany was still on vacation.

Sam and the rest of Zone 56 marched, too. Everyone waved a little American flag. Several of the Zone 56 members joined together to hold up a large banner they made that read "God cleans up LIVES."

Balloons! Banners! Confetti! Drums! Nothing was as fun as a parade!

Afterward there were family picnics at Shawnee Park. Plus lots of splashing at Circleville City Pool. Then everyone watched the fireworks in the high school stadium. It was a perfect ending to a very fun day.

But not an end to the PTs' problems.

For one thing, despite their best precautions, Sam had gotten poison ivy at the lake Saturday while she was picking up trash. Sara was stung by a bumble bee. Sara's dog, Tank, got fleas and infested their whole house with them. Little Noel and Holly were teething, so they cried more than they smiled now — then Jenna's whole family, including the twins, got the stomach flu. Little Lolita's foot still hurt her a lot. Maria broke her new tennis racket, then got blisters marching in the parade. Petie's softball team had lost every game so far. Sara was supposed to get her new braces this summer, but now her doctor said she would have to wait until fall.

And on top of that, they were all bitten by mosquitoes while watching the fireworks that night. Sonya and her dad were scheduled to leave on a week's vacation to visit relatives at the Cherokee Indian reservation. "I'm just itching to get to know them!" she joked as she said good-bye to the PTs after the fireworks, scratching away at the red bites on her arms and legs.

The next day, Sam received her results from the design contest. She hadn't won after all! Not even an honorable mention! The designs she was drawing in class weren't going too well either. She'd hoped to sew herself a zillion new outfits over the summer to make up for the clothes she'd outgrown, but she had yet to make a single one. *Maybe I should just give up,* she thought.

And bad stuff just kept happening! Granny B.'s beautiful tomato plants were attacked by tomato hookworms and shriveled up. LaToya ran over a piece of metal while mowing the lawn so her mower had to go to the shop for repairs. Then Brittany returned from vacation with a sprained ankle!

"Everything is going wrong!" Sam moaned as she and LaToya walked up to Mrs. Greenleaf's to feed the cats. "Why does God let us have troubles, anyway?"

"I don't know, but I sure am praying that it stops soon!" LaToya answered.

The two elderly women were on the porch

fanning themselves. "Hot as a firecracker, don't ya think?" Mrs. Ryan remarked.

"You two feeding those no-good cats again, are you?" Mrs. Greenleaf huffed. "Never did like cats. And not about to start now."

The mother cat was feeding her babies out on the grass under a bush this time. When she saw the girls, she jumped up and hissed. But she didn't run away. Instead, she walked over to her dishes and waited. "Nice kitty," Sam said as she filled up the dishes with cat food and water.

The kittens' eyes were fully open now. Curious, they tried to wobble over to Sam and LaToya. "Oh, look, Mrs. Greenleaf!" Sam said, as the golden one crawled up into her lap. "Aren't they adorable?"

"Mrs. Greenleaf can't see, dear," Mrs. Ryan reminded her. "But they are cute little critters, aren't they?"

"Definitely! I just love holding them and…" Sam stopped. "Sara, I have a great idea that might just solve all our problems." Then she corrected herself, "Well, not all. But at least it might get us to Camp Porcupine!"

Back home, the girls had a quick PTs meeting and Sam shared her idea: a pet care service. For the next three weeks or so, until time for camp, they would do everything possible to help people with their pets. They decided to call their business "Porcupine Pet Pals." Then they made a list of what

they could do:
√ walk dogs
√ care for animals when people are on vacation
√ clean out bird cages
√ clean out rabbit hutches
√ shovel out stables
√ give animals baths

"We could even help with 'doggie' birthday parties down at Bark Park," LaToya added.

"My mom and dad love animals, too," Sara said. "They might be able to draw or paint pictures of people's pets for them."

"And maybe we could buy plain feeding bowls and paint pets' names on them," Jenna suggested.

Sam nodded. "I bet my mom and some of the other animal shelter workers would help us, and my Aunt Caitlin down at her sister's pet shop. We should make signs to hang in vets' offices."

"It'll be a lot of work," Maria decided. "But a lot of fun, too. So does this sound good to everyone?"

"Anything to go to camp," Brittany agreed. "Even if it means 'going to the dogs'!"

· Good News · from God's Word

Here's a Bible story about someone else who found answers to her problems.

Manoah's Wife Finds Hope

FROM JUDGES 13:1-24

God had brought the Israelites out of Egypt, where they were slaves. Those were terrible times, but now they were free. Eventually, they started new lives in beautiful Canaan, just as God had promised them.

But many of the Israelites turned away from God to worship pagan idols. Over 40 years, their cruel Philistine neighbors constantly caused trouble for them with raids and wars. The Israelites cried out to God for help. And God heard their cries.

One Israelite couple was especially sad in those days. Manoah and his wife not only had trouble with the Philistines, but they didn't have the one thing they wanted most: a child of their own. They prayed often for a baby, as well as for help against their oppressors.

Then one day an angel appeared to the woman. "God is going to give you a baby," the angel said. "He is going to be a very special baby who will grow up and deliver your land from the Philistines. But you are not to cut his hair."

The woman rushed to tell her husband. "An angel just spoke to me!" she cried. "And he said we're going to have a baby!"

Manoah could hardly believe it. "Oh, Lord," he prayed, "teach us how to raise this wonderful child You are sending us."

God answered his prayer. Later, they had a baby boy named Samson. The Lord blessed him. And when he grew up, he did become a great hero for the Israelites, just like God's angel had promised.

A Verse to Remember

These three remain: faith, hope and love.
But the greatest of these is love.

— 1 Corinthians 13:13

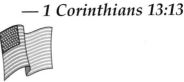

Free to Be Me?

Citizens of the United States have many freedoms guaranteed them by the Constitution. What do the following freedoms mean? Mark your answer for each one. The answers are on page 190.

1. Freedom of the press means:
a. the freedom to iron clothes.

continued on next page...

b. the freedom to publish what you believe.

c. the freedom to publish something and say it's true, even if you know it's a lie.

d. all of the above

2. Freedom of speech means:

a. the freedom to blab anytime and anywhere you want, as loud as you want.

b. the freedom to say mean things to people to their faces.

c. the freedom to say the truth, while trying to be honest, tactful and constructive.

d. all of the above

3. Freedom of worship means:

a. the freedom not to have someone else's religion forced on you.

b. the freedom to attend the church of your choice without being arrested.

c. the freedom to read your Bible and pray.

d. all of the above

4. Freedom of assembly means:

a. the freedom to meet peaceably with others for any lawful purpose.

b. the freedom not to go to school assemblies.

c. the freedom to work on a factory assembly line.

d. all of the above

5. Freedom to petition the government means:

a. the freedom to overthrow the government.

b. the freedom to sue for wrong things done to you.

c. the freedom to own pets.

d. all of the above

6. Freedom to vote means:

a. freedom to buy and sell votes.

b. freedom to turn the nation into a dictatorship.

c. freedom to select leaders.

d. all of the above

Signs of the Times Puzzle

Add the Secret Letter "N" for "not giving up" to space 13 of the puzzle.

Chapter 9

Gross! Weirdos!

That Sunday in Sunday school, Brittany had exciting news to share. "When we were in Florida, I got together with my cousin Nicole. We hadn't seen each other since first grade. We did all the amusement parks together. Anyway, she and her parents decided to come spend some time with us. So I won't be at Zone 56 tonight, because we'll be picking her up at the airport. They've never been here, so it's going to be fun showing her around."

Maria and Le had news, too. "Please pray for us," Maria requested. "We start helping out with the vacation Bible school at Midland tomorrow. We have to be there at 7:30 in the morning. Which means getting up by 6 — with the sun!"

"Plus," Le grinned, "Mom and Mr. Phan got engaged. He says I can call him 'Dad' if I want. But that's going to take a lot of getting used to."

"Wonderful!" Miss Kotter exclaimed. "Have they set a date yet?"

Le shook her head. "Sometime this fall. But little Michael and Nicholas are so cute. They said they always wanted a big sister just like me. Isn't that sweet?"

Sam nodded. "You're going to like being a big sister, Le.

"By the way, we're getting lots of work with our Porcupine Pet Pals. This afternoon I'm going to hamster-sit and rabbit-sit and guinea pig-sit. That family even has pet mice! I'll bet Stormy would have fun with them!" Stormy was Sara's pet cat that her family had rescued during the flood last spring.

After the laughter died down, the girls prayed. Then they opened their Bibles and studied about Pilate's wife. "God helped her know the right thing to do," Miss Kotter explained. "Even when it was hard to do it. God will help you do the right thing, too, if you ask Him. But it won't always be easy. Or popular. Or praised by others. In fact, they might even get angry with you."

That afternoon, LaToya biked over to Mrs.

Greenleaf's to feed the cat. Mrs. Ryan was sitting on the porch by herself. Young hollyhock and sunflower plants grew nearby. This time, the mother cat sniffed LaToya's hand and rubbed against her leg. "I bet she's been someone's pet in the past," Mrs. Ryan said. "Cats can be such good friends. When I was homeless I used to feed a cat behind the store trash bins. I called her Moonlight, because that's the best kind of night for looking in trash bins."

Sighing, she continued. "But a delivery truck ran her over. Well, I sure miss the sweet thing. This mama cat seems awfully nice. If only Mrs. Greenleaf weren't so dead set against her."

LaToya thought for a moment, then smiled. "Mrs. Ryan, if you wheel out Mrs. Greenleaf, maybe she wouldn't mind petting a kitten. What do you think?"

The older woman grinned, too. In a moment she was back with her friend. "OK, Mrs. Greenleaf," LaToya said. "Let's play a game. Close your eyes. I'm going to put something by your cheek. See if you can guess what it is."

"Now, child," the elderly woman retorted, "you know I'm too old to play games. Besides, I can't see." But she smiled and closed her eyes anyway.

"OK, I'm ready."

When LaToya placed the little calico kitten against her cheek, Mrs. Greenleaf cried, "My, that's soft." Then the kitten started purring, and a smile broke out on her wrinkled face. "A kitten! Oh, my! Let me touch it."

LaToya placed it in her hands. "Now, don't you two laugh at me!" she scolded. "I said I can't stand cats. Didn't say nothing about kittens!"

LaToya and Mrs. Ryan could hardly stop giggling.

After Brittany's cousin Nicole arrived in Circleville, she and Brittany sat up half the night talking. Brittany was fascinated with her cousin. She wore her glossy black hair almost as short as a boy's, and she was allowed to wear as much makeup as she wanted. She also had long, dangling earrings, and a butterfly tattoo on one shoulder. Nicole seemed so glamorous and grown-up, just the way Brittany always tried to look.

The next day, Mrs. Boorsma let Nicole borrow her bike. Then Nicole and Brittany rode around Circleville, checking out everything. They rode past Madison Middle School and Circleville High School. Then they swung by Shawnee Park, where Maria and Jenna were practicing tennis, and Sara's big brother was on lifeguard duty.

"He's cute!" Nicole decided. "Let's come back and swim, OK?"

They passed Sam, who was walking four dogs. Then they rode past the mall, the train station, the grain towers and Faith Church.

"I've met the neatest kids there," Brittany said. "And the pastor helped Mom and Dad make up and get back together."

Nicole shrugged. "So what do you do for fun around here?"

"Well, cheerleading and stuff. And at church I play the keyboards for the praise band. And..."

"Church?" Nicole frowned. "Come on, Brittany. How can church be a fun place? Don't you have a teen dance club or cool coffeehouse or someplace where you can really just hang out and meet guys?"

Just then they biked past the rescue mission. Hungry men and women were lined up outside waiting for lunch. Most of them had torn and ragged clothes. Some of the men had long beards.

Nicole shuddered. "Gross! What weirdos! They're creepy! Let's get out of here!"

Just then, Miss Kotter drove up on her lunch hour to drop off some bags of donated clothes.

"Hi, Brittany!" she called, waving her arm. "Who's your friend?"

Nicole stared at her cousin in disgust. "You mean you know someone who comes here?"

Brittany blushed. Suddenly she remembered all the times in the past when she snubbed other people every chance she got. It would be so easy to snub her teacher now, and pretend she didn't hear her. Maybe she was overdoing the church thing. Maybe...

No. That's the way the old Brittany would act. But not God's beloved daughter.

"Hi, Miss Kotter!" she called back. "This is my cousin Nicole from Florida."

The smile on Brittany's face was as big as the one in her heart.

· Good News · from God's Word

This is the Bible story Miss Kotter's class studied.

Pilate's Wife Follows God's Leading

FROM MATTHEW 27:11-26

Pontius Pilate was a very important man, the ruler of most of Israel under the Roman emperor. He was responsible for the soldiers, courts, finances, and especially taxes. He let the Jewish people oversee most of their own courts, but only he could impose the death penalty.

That's why Jesus was brought before Pilate when He was captured. The Jewish leaders wanted Jesus put to death. So they had to convince Pilate that Jesus had done something terribly wrong. This was hard to do, since Jesus had never done anything wrong in His entire life!

When Pilate saw Jesus, he thought Jesus was a quiet, nice sort of person. "People say You're the King of the Jews," he said, jokingly. But it was no joke!

"That's right," Jesus said.

Pilate knew that he was the Jews' leader. He didn't realize Jesus meant that He was their spiritual leader. All of the Jewish leaders kept yelling about how horrible Jesus was. Pilate found that hard to believe. Jesus seemed like such a gentle man! Pilate wanted to let Jesus go, but by this time a great crowd had gathered.

It was the custom to release one prisoner during the Passover holiday, which this was. Pilate had two prisoners: Jesus and Barabbas. Barabbas had been arrested for high treason. "OK," Pilate said, "which prisoner do you want released?" He wanted the people to choose, so he wouldn't have to do it himself.

Just then a servant handed Pilate a note from his wife. "Please," the note read, "don't harm this innocent man. I just had a terrible dream telling me that would be wrong." We don't know if she was a believer or not, but God had sent Pilate's wife this special dream.

She knew the right thing to do, and did it. Her husband knew the right thing to do, too. But he didn't do it. He didn't listen to her. He didn't listen to God. Even though he knew Jesus was falsely accused. Even though he had the power to save Jesus.

He took the easy way out. Pilate sent Jesus to be beaten, then crucified.

A Verse to Remember

Trust in the Lord with all your heart and lean not on your own understanding.

— ***Proverbs 3:5***

What About You?

The Scripture above is one that will help you all your life — when you're afraid, tempted, lonely, confused, discouraged or proud. Yes, God wants you to use the intelligence, talents and skills He gave you. But you will need His help to avoid making many serious mistakes in your life. Always look to God for guidance as you go along.

How could you use God's guidance today? Write your answer below.

_____

_____

_____

Who's Who in This Zoo?

In this puzzle are 4 dogs, 3 cats, 2 turtles, 2 fish, 1 horse, 1 snake, 1 duck, 2 birds, 1 rabbit and 2 mice for the PTs to care for. Can you find them all?

Signs of the Times Puzzle

Add the Secret Letter "H" for "heeding God's Word" to space 7 of the puzzle.

Chapter 10

Shake, Rattle and...

When Sonya and her dad returned from visiting their Cherokee relatives, they brought all sorts of souvenirs with them, including pots, baskets and books about Cherokee history.

"We even went to a powwow on the grounds," she told the PTs. "I couldn't jump around and dance like the other kids, of course. But look what I could do!"

She tied some turtle shell shakers on her arms and shook them. "See, they're like tambourines."

Maria and Le talked Sonya into going with

them to vacation Bible school in Midland the next day so she could share her souvenirs with the children there. Mr. Silverhorse let Pastor Andy borrow his van to drive the girls so there would be room for Sonya's wheelchair.

Petie, Ricardo, Juan, Katie and Suzie were so excited to hear about the Cherokees that they convinced Mrs. Moreno to drive them over, too.

At the Midland VBS, the kids studied the Bible story of Jesus going to the temple when he was 12 years old. Maria and Le helped translate for the children who spoke Spanish or Vietnamese. Some of them belonged to migrant workers' families. Then the teachers encouraged the kids to act out the story.

After the Bible story, the teachers invited Sonya to show her souvenirs and tell about the Cherokee people. Then the whole group sang songs about Jesus while Sonya moved the shakers on her arms in time to the music.

Later, Sonya showed the kids outside what she had learned about wheelchair basketball. "I'm going to be in a tournament in Summer City in two weeks," she explained. "Everyone's invited to come watch."

When Sonya got back home, she was excited. "Sam," she exclaimed, "the VBS kids want to act out today's Bible story about Jesus going to the temple when he was a boy. They want to present it to their parents on the last day of VBS. Can you help me design some costumes for them?"

Sam had just come in from design class. "Me? I'm doing terrible in design, Sonya. I didn't even win an honorable mention in that design contest we entered."

"Well, neither did I, but I know we can do this, working together. And Le volunteered to sew what we design. OK?"

"Well, OK...soon as I give three dogs a flea bath. LaToya and Sara are going to help me. Then we have to walk four more dogs and feed Mrs. Greenleaf's cat."

"I know how to walk dogs," Sonya replied. "I hold on to their leashes like reins of a horse. If they try to wander away, I turn on my wheelchair motor so they have to come with me. If they want to race ahead, I turn off my motor and let them pull me!"

At Mrs. Greenleaf's the four girls played with the kittens while the mother cat ate. This time, Mrs. Greenleaf asked for a kitten to play with, too. Mrs. Ryan caressed the mother cat as she ate. "Nice kitty, nice kitty," she murmured. "I used to have a cat named Moonlight. But I think Starlight is a good name for you."

"We don't need no cat," Mrs. Greenleaf barked. "But we might need a kitten. Mind if I hold another one?" As Sam handed her the white one, Mrs. Greenleaf asked, "Now what you girls snickering about?"

By now the kittens could romp all over. They liked to scamper up on the girls' shoulders and hide under their shirts. "We'll have to find homes for them soon," LaToya decided. "But I sure hate to see them go."

After their pet duties, Sam and Sonya went

back to Sam's house to discuss costumes for the vacation Bible school kids.

When Sam had tried to think up ideas for her design class assignments, it was like pulling teeth. She couldn't think of anything! But now that she was working with Sonya, suddenly all kinds of clever ideas started flowing out of her brain. She started coming up with good designs not just for the costumes but for her class, too. Maybe it was because instead of thinking about fancy formals and wedding gowns, she had camp on her brain. Camp Porcupine was coming quickly and she had absolutely nothing to wear! So after Sonya left, Sam dashed to her room to start sketching easy, but cute, camp clothes.

That evening, Pastor Andy called the Zone 56 members and the other Faith Church youth groups together for a quick meeting. He wanted to plan a Splash Bash for Friday night at Shawnee Park.

"Tony's a lifeguard there this summer," he explained, "so he's going to help us, too." Brittany had brought Nicole to the meeting. Even though Nicole was down on church activities, she brightened when she heard about Tony's participation. "Lucky I brought my best bathing suit!" she whispered happily to Brittany.

Home in bed that night, Sam thought about all her PTs and what they had done that day. Especially what they had done for the Lord. "Jesus was right," she told Sneezit as she gave him an extra cuddle. "He was old enough to work for the Lord. And so are we!"

· Good News · from God's Word

This is the Bible story the children studied in vacation Bible school.

Jesus Is Old Enough for God's Work

FROM LUKE 2:41-52

Mary and Joseph lived in Nazareth with their family. Nazareth was up in the hill country of Galilee, only about 60 miles or so from Jerusalem. Today, the trip takes no time at all. But in those days people walked or rode donkeys from place to place. Walking 60 miles would take a long time! But the people made the trip every year for the Passover Feast, as did thousands of other people from all over the country.

By the time Jesus was 12, Mary had several younger children to care for. But by this age Jesus was old enough to have lots of friends His own age, just like kids today. So whenever He wasn't around His parents and the rest of His family, they didn't worry. They figured He was with His friends.

When the feast was over, Mary and Joseph and their children packed up for the long trip home. They traveled with a large group of friends and family from Nazareth. Even though Mary and Joseph couldn't see Jesus among them, Mary said, "Oh, well, He and His friends must be walking together."

But by that evening, they still didn't see Him. Where in the world could He be?, they wondered. They checked with all His friends, but no one had seen Him. It was too late for them to travel alone that night back to Jerusalem. So the next morning they headed back. By now they must have been very worried.

They had walked north toward home for one whole day. Then they walked back south for another whole day. Now they spent a whole day looking for Him, becoming more frightened by the moment.

Mary and Joseph looked in the stores, the streets, the parks and the government buildings. Finally, they found Him in the temple, sitting with a circle of old Bible teachers and asking them questions. Yet He was also giving answers — just like one of them. Mary and Joseph were astonished.

"Oh, Jesus!" Mary cried. "We've been frantic! We've looked everywhere for You!"

"Why didn't you look for Me here in the first place?" Jesus replied. "Didn't you know I would be in My Father's house?"

Jesus obediently went home with His parents. And the Bible says that Mary continued to reflect in awe on what had happened.

A Verse to Remember

This Scripture is what Jesus told His parents when they found Him. Even though he was only 12, Jesus knew that God had work for Him to do. God has special plans for you, too.

Didn't you know I had to be in my Father's house?
— Luke 2:49

What About You?

Is there something you could be doing for the Lord? Something special? Pray about it. Talk to your pastor or Sunday school teacher about what it might be. Remember, you're not too young, just as Jesus wasn't. Write some ideas below:

_____

_____

_____

_____

Absolutely Nothing to Wear

Do you go to camp in the summer? Or are there other fun activities you like to do in the summer? In the picture below, either draw some camp clothes on Sam or draw an outfit for what you like to do.

Signs of the Times Puzzle

Add the Secret Letter "E" for "eternity-minded" to space 8 of the puzzle.

Chapter 11

Splash Bash

After checking with each PT family, Sonya and Sam located enough old towels, sheets and fabric strips to work with. Then they completed the Bible costumes in record time.

Sam gave Sonya a high-five. "We did it!" she exulted. "And this has given me all kinds of ideas for camp clothes. In fact, when I showed my sketches of them to my design teacher, her eyes really lit up. She said they were my best work so far."

Sonya smiled. "That's great. I've been designing some, too – not just for camp but for the basketball tournament. How about we team up and help each other out? Oh, by the way, do we need to be planning snacks for the Splash Bash?"

"I think Pastor Andy's picking up a bunch of burgers and fries. As to working with you on designs, you're on, partner." Giggling, she added, "And let's hope we don't eat so many burgers and fries Friday night that our new clothes are already too tight the first time we wear them!"

Meanwhile, Sara and Jenna walked some dogs over to the Bark Park for their Porcupine Pet Pals fund-raising. On the way, they passed Brittany and Nicole on their bikes.

"Hi, Brit!" Sara called. "Hi, Nicole! You look like you're having fun."

"Anytime you want to play doubles with Maria and me, let us know," Jenna added. "And don't forget the Splash Bash Friday night. You're invited, too, Nicole."

Just then Brittany glanced at her watch. "Oops! Almost forgot. It's my turn to feed the cat. We gotta go, Nicole. 'Bye, guys."

Nicole grinned slyly as they rode off. "Oh, I get it. You don't really have a cat. So you just pretended you did to get away from them, right?"

"No! All of the PTs are helping take care of a

cat at Mrs. Greenleaf's. The cat had kittens a few weeks ago under Mrs. Greenleaf's porch. You'll love playing with them."

And Nicole did. The golden one kissed her on the ear. The black one ran up a tree and meowed piteously for someone to help him down. The calico one grabbed a shoestring on Nicole's sneakers and pulled on it with all her might. Mrs. Greenleaf happily cuddled one of the gray-striped kittens. The other two ran around.

After finishing her own meal, the mother cat called to them. The kittens began eating and nestling up to her as close as possible.

"They're really getting big," Brittany sighed on their way home. "We'll have to find them homes soon."

Nicole looked puzzled. "I don't get it, Cuz. I mean, those kittens are cute and all that. But those old ladies – how can you stand being around them? Life's supposed to be fun. Old ladies and church stuff and rescue missions aren't fun. It all gives me the creeps. That's not the Brittany who used to write me. You used to be so cool. And now even your parents go to church. I mean, you've all done a big 180. What happened?"

Brittany didn't know what to say. She wanted to burst out with, "Look, Nicole, we're talking serious business here. I almost died. God saved my life. And He gave me love and new life in Jesus. And two wonderful pets. And lots of friends. And made us all a family again."

But if Nicole already thought she wasn't cool, that would cinch it, Brittany decided. So instead, she smiled brightly. "Hey, ready for some lemonade? And some video games? I've got dibs on the red controller. You want purple or pink?" In her heart she prayed God would give her another chance to talk to her cousin about spiritual things — and the courage to do it.

On Friday morning, the Bible play at vacation Bible school was a great success. Mrs. Moreno drove her boys plus Petie, Katie and Suzie back to Midland again for it. Maria had never seen them so impressed about God's Word! She and Le gave Shannon a good hug before they left and said they'd see her that night. Their pastor had promised to bring their youth group over to Circleville for the Splash Bash.

That evening, almost all of Faith Church's youth group members showed up for the Splash Bash. Plus all the Midland kids! Sonya, wearing special plastic floats, had fun in the water along with the rest of the crowd. They played tag and Marco Polo, tossed a beach ball and raced from one end of the pool to the other. After a whole string of blistering, rainless days, the cool water felt absolutely marvelous.

Nicole had as much fun as anyone. Being from Florida where she could swim almost year-round, Nicole was a good swimmer. She was fearless on the diving board! Even Tony, Sara's big brother, had a hard time holding his own with her. "Any time you want a lifeguard job," he teased, "come on back to Circleville."

Afterward, the group sat at picnic tables under the Shawnee Park trees for burgers and fries. Then LaToya played her guitar while Pastor Andy led some songs. After that he talked about Jesus and finding peace and joy and purpose in Him.

Nicole was quiet on their way back to Brittany's. Finally, she confided, "Your friends are really neat, Brittany. But I kinda got lost in what that Andy guy was talking about. Could you clue me in a bit?"

Thank You, God! Brittany prayed silently. Then she said, "Sure, Nicole. See, here's how it all began…"

· Good News ·
from God's Word

Brittany isn't the only one who has had problems sometimes being a good witness for Christ. So did the apostle Peter!

Two Girls Look to Peter for an Answer
FROM MATTHEW 26:21-75

Peter loved Jesus. Jesus was kind to him. He loved traveling around the country with Jesus, listening to Him tell people about God. He was thrilled to see Jesus do miracles. He couldn't wait until Jesus was King of the whole nation. Then everyone would think good thoughts and do good things. For Jesus was the promised Messiah!

One evening Jesus and His disciples celebrated Passover together. But Jesus told them something sad. "Tonight," He said, "you will all leave me. Peter will disown me three times before the morning rooster crows."

"Oh, no! Never!" Peter cried. He couldn't even imagine denying Him!

That night, a huge crowd armed with clubs and swords captured Jesus and dragged him away. They took him to the high priests and other religious leaders. They asked Him questions, hit Him and made fun of Him.

Peter waited outside in the courtyard, not knowing what was going to happen. One young servant girl came by and saw Peter. "Oh, you're one of Jesus' disciples, aren't you?" she asked.

Peter was scared. "I don't know what you're talking about!" he shouted.

He walked away. But then another girl saw him. "He's one of Jesus' disciples," she said.

"No!" he yelled. "I don't know the man!"

He said the same thing to someone else. Then he heard the rooster crow. Jesus was right. Peter had denied Him three times. Peter missed an opportunity to tell those two girls about His Savior.

Peter felt so bad, the Bible says, he went off and wept bitterly.

A Verse to Remember

Whoever acknowledges me before men,
I will also acknowledge him
before my Father in heaven.

— Matthew 10:32

What About You?

Do you have trouble telling people you believe in Christ? Of course, that's usually not hard to do at church. But what about at school? In your family? When you hang out with your friends? Write below the names of people you want to tell about Jesus, then think about how you will do it.

_____

_____

_____

Singing About Jesus

Here's a song to sing to the tune of "Mary Had a Little Lamb." It helps tell others about Jesus. Try jazzing it up with a Caribbean beat!

Jesus is my favorite friend, favorite friend, favorite friend.
Jesus is my favorite friend. He'll always be, I know.

He follows me to school each day,
school each day, school each day.
He follows me to school each day, and everywhere I go.

He helps me at my work and play,
work and play, work and play.
He helps me at my work and play. He's always at my side.

He is my Savior, He's my Lord, He's my Lord,
He's my Lord.
He is my Savior, He's my Lord. For me in love He died.

That's why He is my favorite friend, favorite friend,
favorite friend.
That's why He is my favorite friend —
and will be to the end!

Signs of the Times Puzzle

Add the Secret Letter "O" for "openly confessing Him" to space 19 of the puzzle.

Chapter 12

Dollars and Sense

Nicole returned home to Florida on Saturday morning. "Circleville is not as exciting as Florida," Nicole told Brittany before she left. "But I had a great time. And I'm going to ask my mom if we can get a kitten when I get back."

Brittany gave her a hug. "Look for a church, too, OK? And give me a call or an e-mail as soon as you get home. We've got to keep in touch."

Later that morning the PTs had a quick business meeting. Subject: money. Specifically, money collected so far to pay for Camp Porcupine for everyone.

"What we need," Sara said, "is $525. That's $75 for each of us."

"Well, not really," Sam broke in. "My Aunt Caitlin just told me she'd pay my way because I've been babysitting Suzie for her."

"And Mom and Dad said they can pay for me," Brittany added.

Sara did some quick erasing. "OK, I stand corrected. So now we need $375. That's still a lot of money!"

"I've been saving up all spring," Sonya said. "I've got $70 now. I get $5 allowance a week. So this week's $5 should do it for me."

More erasing. "Well, now we're down to $300."

"How much in our Porcupine Pet Pals fund so far?" Jenna asked.

Sara began counting the money they had earned. "I've walked so many dogs lately I've started catching balls with my teeth!" LaToya teased.

Maria giggled. "Come on, get serious. What's the total?"

Sara smiled. "We have a grand total of…drum roll, please…$269.50!"

Sam sighed in relief. "That means only $30.50 left to go. And we still have all next week to get it. We'll be able to make it by the time we leave a week from Sunday."

Total: $269.50

Suddenly Jenna gasped. "Wait a minute. Didn't Pastor Andy say all the money had to be in by this Sunday?"

LaToya groaned. "That's right! We're supposed to hand it in at the Zone 56 meeting tomorrow night. Now what do we do?"

"Well, we still have this afternoon," Maria said. "What's something we could do real quick for money?"

"A car wash!" Sam and Le yelled at once.

So that's how they spent the afternoon — at a car wash in the church parking lot. First they called the church custodian and got permission to use the lot. He said they were welcome to hold the car wash there as long as they promised to clean up afterward. Then they called Kevin and Josh from Zone 56. Even though they already had their own money for camp, the guys and their friends all agreed to help. They couldn't pass up a chance to spray water and throw sponges at the PTs!

After a hot June with no rain, most Circleville cars were very dusty, so business was brisk. By the time they shut down that afternoon, they had made over $150.

"Enough and some to spare! Yeah!" Sonya said. "Now what should we do with the extra money?"

"Let's pray about it," Maria suggested. After they cleaned up the mess in the parking lot, the PTs gathered for a short prayer to thank God for helping them achieve their goal. They also asked for His guidance in spending the extra money.

As Maria walked in her front door, the phone

rang. It was Shannon.

"Hi, Shannon!" Maria cried. "Guess what? We just had a car wash to raise money for church camp. So now we all can go. What about you?"

Shannon was quiet a minute. "That's what I was calling about, Maria. My mom was sick and off work a couple days last week. She doesn't get sick pay, so we'll be short this month. I guess I won't see you at camp, after all."

After she ended her call with Shannon, Maria didn't hang up the phone. Instead, she quickly called all of the PTs to tell them about Shannon. Everyone agreed on where the extra car wash money should go: to Shannon!

"So you don't get out of camp after all, Shannon," Maria teased when she called Shannon a few minutes later. "And as soon as I get there, I'm going to beat you at tennis."

· Good News ·
from God's Word

Here's a Bible story about someone else who gave from her heart.

Susanna Gives from Her Heart

FROM LUKE 8:1-3

Jesus grew up learning how to be a carpenter. He and his brothers and sisters helped in Joseph's carpentry shop. They learned how to saw and nail and sand and fit wood pieces together just right. Because many homes were built from stone in Nazareth, it is possible that Jesus also learned to work with stone, metal and other materials. His family never became wealthy, but it was good, honest work that helped them make a living.

When Jesus was 30 years old, God called Him to do something else: to preach God's gospel of peace and love. Soon other men joined Him to travel around the country preaching and healing. We call them Jesus' disciples.

Obviously, Jesus couldn't travel around preaching and also stay home working in His carpentry shop. So instead of working for His food, He needed friends to help provide food for Him and His disciples.

Jesus never asked anyone to help Him. But there were some women who had been very sick and Jesus healed them. After that, they couldn't do enough for Him. Three of those women were Mary Magdalene, Joanna and Susanna. The Bible says there were also many others. These women decided that God wanted them to provide food and shelter for Jesus and His disciples.

We don't know anything else about Susanna. We don't know whether she was old or young, married or unmarried, rich or poor. But we do know she loved Jesus and gave generously to show that love. Do people know that about you?

A Verse to Remember

It is more blessed to give than to receive.

— Acts 20:35

What About You?

You might get a large allowance, a small allowance or no allowance at all. Maybe you babysit or do other chores for your own family and for others to get extra money. How wisely do you use that money? There are always clothes, movies, snacks, video games and many other things to spend it on. But how much do you give to your church and to help others?

Even if you have no money, you can still give to others. Do the word search puzzle on the next page and see how. Maybe you'll discover that you're poor in money, but rich in other things to give.

Signs of the Times Puzzle

Add the Secret Letter "G" for "generous" to space 18 of the puzzle.

Gifts You Can Give

Listed on the next page are 35 things you can give others to bring them joy in life. There are also some things you can give to God. See if you can find all the words in the puzzle. Note that "excuses," "a hard time" and "sassy remarks" are not included! The solution is on page 191.

Word List

Advice	Aid	Appreciation	Approval
Compliments	Courtesy		Credit
Encouragement	Energy		Gifts
Help	Helping Hand		Hope
Hugs	Ideas	Instruction	Kindness
Kisses	Listening	Love	Money
Nods	Opinion	Patience	Pats
Praise	Skills	Smiles	Sympathy
Talents	Thanks	Time	Tips
Toys	Worship		

```
S  A  S  L  I  S  T  E  N  I  N  G  T  Y
T  P  T  X  S  E  A  M  O  G  T  W  N  S
A  P  N  Y  Y  S  I  O  D  I  I  O  E  E
P  R  E  H  O  I  D  N  S  F  P  R  M  T
D  O  M  T  T  A  L  E  N  T  S  S  E  R
N  V  I  A  I  R  X  Y  X  S  M  H  G  U
A  A  L  P  M  P  S  A  E  D  I  I  A  O
H  L  P  M  E  N  E  R  G  Y  L  P  R  C
G  S  M  Y  X  A  D  V  I  C  E  L  U  S
N  K  O  S  X  S  K  I  L  L  S  E  O  S
I  N  C  R  X  X  X  E  P  O  H  H  C  E
P  A  O  P  I  N  I  O  N  V  X  X  N  N
L  H  U  G  S  P  A  T  I  E  N  C  E  D
E  T  N  O  I  T  C  U  R  T  S  N  I  N
H  S  E  S  S  I  K  T  I  D  E  R  C  I
A  P  P  R  E  C  I  A  T  I  O  N  X  K
```

Chapter 13

Work, Work, Work!

The next week, Sam and Sonya worked every possible moment on their new clothes. Sonya wanted something that she could use for her basketball uniform and for camp. It needed to be easy to move around in, but look good enough to wear after camp. Sam wanted cool, comfortable outfits for camp and the rest of summer — something colorful that might also get her an A in design class.

All of the PTs also had to finish up their Porcupine Pet Pals responsibilities.

Sam was still babysitting Suzie and Petie. Petie was on a baseball team, so she had to make sure to get him to all of the practices and games. Then in the evening she practiced volleyball with Sara to get ready for their favorite sport at camp.

"Sam," her mom said in a concerned voice, "I think you're doing too much. Slow down, or you'll get sick. There's a bug going around, you know."

"I'm fine," Sam assured her. "By next week, design class will be over and I'll be at camp."

"But you're not even eating right, Sam. You're just snacking all day long."

"I said I was fine. A few more days and this will be all over."

Sonya was worried about her, too. "Hey, I already have a mother," Sam snapped. "I'm almost done with everything. Then I can relax. So bug off, OK?"

Sam was even mean to Miss Kotter. "Look, I'm a big girl. Thanks, but I can take care of myself. After all, I'm doing all this for God. Doesn't that count?"

Great, Sam thought sarcastically. *First I get fussed at for not working hard enough, and now they're giving me grief for working too hard. I can't win!*

Soon she was even snapping at poor Sneezit. He crawled behind the coach and whimpered.

But she did it! She finished her outfits, ironed them all and hung them up on hangers. She'd have to walk to design class the next day instead of biking so she could carry her clothes. But she couldn't wait until her class saw what she'd done, especially when she modeled everything!

The next morning, though, Sam could hardly move. Her eyes were glazed and the room seemed to spin around when she tried to stand up. Her head felt like a brick and her eyes burned.

Her mom stuck a thermometer into her mouth. "You have a fever, Sam. No design school for you today, young lady."

"But it's the last day of class!" she protested weakly. "I've gotta go. I've got to take my clothes in for a grade. And besides, this afternoon is Sonya's tournament. I can't just stay home in bed."

"I'm afraid you have to, Sam. You're in no shape to do anything. Besides, you'd just infect everyone else with whatever you have. I'll drop off your clothes at your class on my way to work and pick them up on my way home. As for you, you're going to take some aspirin, have a nice cool bath and go right back to bed."

What a miserable day to stay home! Petie was at the Morenos, playing with Ricardo and Juan. Mrs. Moreno brought Sam some soup, but she couldn't even look at it. Her stomach was too upset to consider food.

It's not fair, God! she whined. I worked so hard. I've tried to do everything right. So why did You let me get sick? Why did You let me miss my big day at design school? And Sonya's tournament? I promised her I'd go. And now I'm letting her down!

Sam nibbled on a cracker. She took a couple of

sips from a water bottle. Then she lay down on the couch to watch TV, but promptly fell asleep.

Her mom woke her up when she stopped by on her lunch hour. "Here are your outfits back," she said. "I'll hang them up in your closet. Miss Garry said you get an A+! She especially liked this sundress you made for camp chapel services. Aren't you thrilled that you did so well?"

Now Sam felt worse than ever. "And I got gypped out of being there to hear what she said! It just isn't fair! I don't think God likes me any more," she whimpered.

"Sam! How can you say something like that?" her mom asked. "You just haven't been taking care of yourself. Now I have to go back to work. Try to get some rest so you'll be up to eating dinner tonight."

Sam dozed off again. Suddenly the phone woke her. "Sam, it's me, Sonya. Guess what? Our team won! I'm so excited! Dad took the afternoon off work and videotaped the whole thing. I'll play it for you when you feel better."

"That's great, Sonya. Sure, I'd love to see it."

Of course, she would have liked even more to have been there for the real thing!

By the time everyone was home that evening, Sam's fever was almost gone. She still wasn't up to eating dinner. But she was up to thinking about a lot of things.

"Please forgive me for blaming You, God," she prayed. "And help me next time to pace myself so I don't get sick and miss out on the fun!"

· Good News · from God's Word

God was glad for Sam to work hard for Him. But He also wanted her to take care of herself. Here are some more Bible women who worked hard for the Lord.

Persis and Friends Work for the Lord

FROM ROMANS 16:12

Did you ever move from one home to another? Maybe you moved within the same city. Or maybe you moved all the way across the country or the world!

People did that in Paul's day, too. Paul himself traveled from city to city and country to country telling people about Jesus. Many people heard and believed in Jesus because of Paul. They started new churches. Then some of them moved to other cities or countries where they spread the gospel about God's Son to still others, and started even more churches.

That's why Paul, in his letter to the Romans, addressed so many old friends even though he had never been to Rome himself. For instance, in his letter he sends greetings to Aquila and Priscilla and to the new church meeting in their home.

He sends his love to many other Christians, old and new, including Persis, Tryphena, Tryphosa and Mary. (This was another Mary, not any of those we find other places in the Bible.) He commends all these women for working hard for the Lord and His people. He says that Persis has "worked very hard in the Lord." He wrote this letter to them and to all Christians in Rome so they would know to not just do the work themselves, but to let God's Holy Spirit do His work through them.

This wasn't easy, of course — not in a huge pagan city like Rome where just being a Christian might put one's life at risk. But they were glad to work hard for God and for each other.

Later, Paul was able to go to Rome and thank them all in person.

 A Verse to Remember

Walk in the way of understanding.

— *Proverbs 9:6*

What About You?

Most of us are quick to give advice...but slow to take it. What about you? Would you rather rush ahead, doing things your own way and risk making mistakes? Or would you rather listen to the counsel of those who love you, such as teachers, pastors, parents, grandparents, doctors and friends? As the old saying goes, "Experience is a great teacher, but learning from someone else's experience is even better"!

Write about a time below when you took someone's advice rather than doing it your own way:

_____

_____

_____

Working Smart

Doing your best is always important. But sometimes our best isn't what we think it is. If Sam had taken the time to eat right and get some rest while doing all her work, she might not have gotten sick. See if you can help the PTs in the situations on the next page to work smarter, not harder, by saving time and energy to achieve the same good results. Circle your answer, then check page 191 and grade yourself. Did you get an A+? If not, practice working smarter rather than harder in your own life.

1. Sonya needs to take her school books and supplies from the living room to her bedroom. She should:

a. Wheel them over one at a time.

b. Carry several at a time, using a tray or bags on her wheelchair.

2. Sam needs to prepare a snack for Petie and Suzie. She should:

a. Make something they both like.

b. Ask Petie what he wants and fix it for him, then ask Suzie what she wants.

3. Jenna is helping her mom with the babies' laundry. She should:

a. Carry the clean clothes by armfuls from the laundry room to the nursery.

b. Fold the clothes in the laundry room, then wheel them all at once to the nursery using the laundry cart.

4. Miss Kotter is helping with grocery shopping for the rescue mission. She should:

a. Buy all the food at once and carry it to the rescue mission at the same time.

b. Buy all the meat and take it to the rescue mission, then return to the store for the other food.

5. Sara has offered to walk her dog, Tank, and Sonya's dog, Cocky. She should:

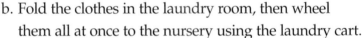

a. Walk each dog separately.

b. Walk the two dogs together, being careful to keep their leashes from tangling.

6. Maria is having an ice cream party for her PTs. She should:

a. Make each cone or sundae in the kitchen, then serve each one separately.

b. Set out the ice cream and toppings and let each girl make her own.

7. Brittany wants obedience training for her dogs, Sweetie and Hope. She should:

a. Take Sweetie through the classes by herself, then Hope.

b. Ask a friend to help her take both dogs through the classes.

8. LaToya is watering Mrs. Greenleaf's lawn. She should:

a. Water it all by hand.

b. Water what she can by using sprinklers.

9. Le needs to carry her violin, bow, music book and all her other books to school. She should:

a. Carry the violin and bow in her violin case, and the rest in her backpack.

b. Carry the violin in one hand and the bow in another. Then make another trip with the rest.

Signs of the Times Puzzle

Add the Secret Letter "T" for "thinking things through" to space 6 of the puzzle.

Chapter 14

Off to Camp

That Saturday, the girls took care of their last promised Porcupine Pet Pals responsibilities, which resulted in $50. Since they had already paid for camp, they split the money eight ways for $5 each. Then they set the rest aside to put in the church offering the next day. After that, they all went to see Mrs. Greenleaf and Mrs. Ryan. And, of course, those darling kittens. Mrs. Greenleaf's lawn needed watering again. The PTs were pleasantly surprised to see that the sunflowers they planted were blooming beautifully.

When Jenna placed some food out for the cat family, the mother cat encouraged her kittens to eat the dry food along with her. "She's starting to wean them," Sam explained. Most of the kittens just sniffed the strange stuff curiously. But the black kitten rushed up and started gulping it down as fast as he could.

"Look at Midnight go!" Sonya joked.

"Wait a minute," Jenna cautioned. "We shouldn't name them. We have to give them away, you know."

"Who said we can't name them?" Brittany objected. "Mrs. Ryan has already named the mother Starlight. So this black one can be Midnight. And the white one is Snow White."

Sara got into the swing of things. "Then the gold one is Sunlight — Sunny, for short."

"Twilight is one of the gray ones," decided LaToya.

That left the calico and other gray one. They finally settled on "Dinah-Mite" and "Skeeter Bite."

Maria sighed. "It's sure going to be hard letting them go."

Sam nodded. "The shelter will make sure they have good homes to go to." Then she clapped her hands together. "Hey, we could give them those good homes ourselves. I mean, if our parents let us. Sara already has Stormy, but none of the rest of us has a kitten."

"Well, if Mom says it's OK, I get dibs on Midnight," Le decided.

Brittany's mom was allergic to cats, so she couldn't have one. But the others quickly divvied them up. The golden Sunlight would be Sam's; the calico Dinah-Mite would be Maria's; Snow White, Sonya's; and the grays, Twilight and Skeeter Bite, would be LaToya's and Jenna's respectively.

"But how can we take them home?" LaToya asked. "We're all leaving for camp tomorrow."

"We can leave them here 'til we come back," Jenna pointed out. "Then Mrs. Pearson can help us get them their shots. And get the mama cat shots and neutered, too."

Sam thought a minute. "That's all going to take money. So more Porcupine Pet Pals when we get back, girls."

By then Mrs. Greenleaf had wheeled out onto the porch, along with Mrs. Ryan.

"Could you feed them all 'til we get back from camp?" Le asked Mrs. Ryan. "Then we can take the babies to their new homes."

"What?" Mrs. Greenleaf cried. "You're taking my kitties away?"

"Now, Norma," Mrs. Ryan protested, "you know your eyes aren't good enough to take care of the little ones. And my legs aren't fast enough to run after them. But their mama is just the right age for old ladies like you and me."

As if on cue, Moonlight jumped up on Mrs. Greenleaf's wheelchair. She leaned against the elderly woman, then settled down in her lap, purring loudly.

"Well, now, don't that beat all?" she cried. Beaming broadly, she started to stroke its fur.

Then frowning, she added, "Now this doesn't mean I like cats. But I guess I can make an exception for this one."

That evening all the PTs who'd picked out kittens asked their parents if they could keep them. All their parents said "yes" — as long as they remembered to take care of them.

The next morning in Sunday school, the PTs studied nine Bible girls who loved animals, just as they did. "We must never consider animals more important than people," Miss Kotter said. "But God does want us to treat them wisely, lovingly and gently. He wants us to appreciate them and to take care of them.

"You girls will see many wild animals at camp," she continued. "You'll see squirrels, chipmunks, raccoons, birds, and maybe even a coyote  or a deer or two. Know and respect the difference between tame animals and wild ones. Wild ones have to find their own food and protect their young. So they can be dangerous to people. Also, they may carry diseases. So enjoy looking at them, listen to them, take their pictures. But save your petting for your dogs, cats and other tame animals."

Then they all talked about camp. Miss Kotter would be one of the volunteer workers there. Others would be Mr. Talley and Miss Temple, two of the Madison teachers; Mr. Silverhorse, Sonya's dad; and

Pastor Andy.

During morning worship, Pastor McConahan asked all of the middle school and high school kids who were going to camp to come to the front of the sanctuary, along with the adult volunteers. Then the whole church prayed for them all.

"Don't forget to pack insect repellent," Sam's mom told her that afternoon. "Plus sunscreen, lots of socks and a beach towel. Your Bible and a notebook, too. And pens and pencils."

Petie came into Sam's bedroom, grinning. "And bring me home a bouquet of these," he teased, holding up a picture he had drawn.

His big sister laughed. "Petie! That's poison ivy!"

Later that afternoon, everyone met at the church for rides to camp. Instead of riding in big yellow school buses as they did to Winter Camp, these campers would travel in cars, vans and trucks.

"Camp Porcupine is up by Monder Mountain, near the school campgrounds," Pastor Andy explained to the drivers. "I've got maps here for everyone. You can caravan along with me, or go at your own speed. See everyone at camp!"

"Camp Porcupine, huh?" Petie repeated as he waved to Sam. "Well, if you get 'stuck' up there, Sam, I get your room!"

Petie laughed so hard at his own joke, he got the hiccups!

· Good News · from God's Word

Here are some of the people the girls studied in Miss Kotter's class that Sunday.

Nine Girls Who Loved Animals

FROM GEN. 24:15-25; 29:1-12; EX. 2:15-21

Since the beginning of time, people have loved animals. Adam and Eve learned to understand and appreciate animals in the Garden of Eden. Adam named all the animals. He and Eve lived in harmony with their beastly friends.

As time went on, many families raised donkeys, cattle, sheep, and goats — even camels. These animals provided transportation, wool, milk, cheese and meat.

Many people also raised pigeons and other birds. But they couldn't let their tame animals wander around unprotected. They might be eaten by wild animals or stolen by other people, or they might get lost or hurt or hungry!

Someone needed to take care of the animals. Often that was the boy or man of the family — such as the singer David. Other times it was girls who had the responsibility. Rebekah was one such girl. Rachel was another. Zipporah and her six sisters were still others.

Sometimes we think of these Bible women only as grown-up mothers and wives. But they were busy working at very important jobs long before that. They needed to find good pastures for their animals, even if it was up a steep hill far from home. They had to find clean, safe water for them at least twice each day, either from a spring or a well or a stream. They needed to find shade for them to rest under when the sun was scorching hot. And then they had to bring them home again safely at night, without any of the animals getting lost.

These shepherdesses worked hard to take care of their animals. God is happy when we care for our animals today, too, and use their resources wisely.

A Verse to Remember

*A righteous man cares for
the needs of his animal.*

— Proverbs 12:10

What About You?

Do you have a pet or pets? If so, write their name or names here:

_____

_____

_____

What do you need to do regularly to take proper care of your pet or pets? How often? Do you remember to do that regularly? If not, ask God to help you keep up with your responsibility.

Pet Shop

Match the numbered rhyming clues with the correct pets below. The answers are on page 191.

A. guinea pig   B. horse   C. mouse

D. cat   E. canary   F. rabbit

G. parrot   H. lizard   I. goldfish   J. dog

1. When I'm glad, I wag my tail
   And bark, so you'll know all is well.

2. I can meow and I can purr
   And let you pet my silky fur.

3. I swim in a glass bowl up and down.
   But please don't worry; I won't drown.

4. "Polly want a cracker?" I can squawk.
   Did you know that some birds can talk?

5. At thinking things through I'm not a wizard.
   Still it's fun to be a _____.

6. My ears are long, my tail is small.
   I like carrots and lettuce and clover, all.

7. You can ride on my back all day.
   Will I buck you off it? Neigh!

8. I'm yellow and sing a lovely song.
   In fact, I'm singing all day long.

9. With long tail and whiskers, I'm small as can be.
   Don't let your kitty play with me.

10. I'm not too small and not too big.
    I'm a round, plump _____.

Signs of the Times Puzzle

Add the Secret Letter "D" for "dealing kindly with animals" to space 11 of the puzzle.

142

Chapter 15

Porc-ing Out

"Welcome to Camp Porcupine!" the camp director called on a megaphone from the parking lot as cars, vans and trucks pulled up, full of campers. "Grab your bags and come on up Quill Hill to Porc Palace."

The campers tumbled out. Pine trees towered overhead. Down below, Sunset Lake glistened under blue skies. Through the trees, they could glimpse Monder (also known as "Monster") Mountain. The campgrounds where they went for Winter Camp last January were around the hillside, just out of sight.

Although this area was higher in altitude than Circleville, and it was already evening, the air outside was uncomfortably warm — especially climbing up the short but steep hillside with sleeping bags, suitcases and other supplies. But inside the main meeting hall, the campers were greeted by a blast of air conditioning and a spread of sandwiches, apples, lemonade and ice cream bars.

"Before we eat, let's thank God for our food and for the great week ahead of us," the director said. "One of the great results of Christian camp is the wonderful new friends you'll make. So let's start making them right now by reaching out and holding hands as we pray."

Sam grabbed Sara's and Sonya's hands. She looked around and smiled. Yes, she was going to make as many new friends as possible, starting right now! *Help me to do it, please, God*, she prayed.

After the prayer, Sam looked around at the hungry crowd. "Oh, Sara!" she exclaimed. "There's Shannon Hendricks! Plus all those kids we met from Midland!"

Sara waved and caught Shannon's eye. "Sara!" Shannon called. "Come on and sit at our table." Just like that, Sara ran across the room. Without a second glance at Sam!

"Well! What do you think about that?" Sam huffed to Sonya. But just then Sonya started waving madly. "Look, Sam! I can't believe it! It's Maddie

Wilson. I was in the wheelchair tournament at Summer City with her this week. I didn't even know she was coming!" And off she wheeled to see her friend.

Sam looked around for the rest of her PTs. Maria and Le had joined the Midland gang, too. After working with many of them during their vacation Bible school, they were eager to renew friendships. Brittany had discovered a friend of hers from cheerleading camp, Jessica Michaels, who lived in Elmwood. LaToya was already deep in discussions about camp music with Pastor Andy and the camp pianist. Jenna was busy talking to Miss Kotter and Miss Temple.

Just a minute! Sam thought with a huff. *None of them are talking to me! I'm not even being missed! Fine friends they have all turned out to be! Is this the way the whole week is going to be? They were supposed to be my PTs!*

As Sam moved along the food line she was so busy feeling left-out that she almost missed hearing something. "Uh, hello-o-o?" repeated the girl behind her, "Didn't you hear me? I asked if you are with the Circleville group."

She turned around. A short girl with coal black curls and twinkly green eyes smiled eagerly. "I'm Colleen O'Riley. I go to Memorial Church in Summer City. I'll bet you're Sam, aren't you? I can tell by your blond ponytail. Ric Romero's told me all about you guys. It's good to finally meet you! You've got to let me introduce you to our whole gang from Memorial over there."

Sam brightened. "Oh, you know Ric? That's great! We miss him so much!"

Suddenly she felt all warm inside. Someone had been friendly to her! Then she thought, *Why wasn't I the one who was friendly to Colleen? I just asked God to help me be friendly to others. And right off I forgot. Please forgive me, dear God. I'll try to do better next time.*

"Oh, it's good to meet you, Colleen. I'd love to meet all your friends — as soon as I fill my dinner tray!"

As the campers finished eating, the camp director grabbed the mike up front. "Hi, everyone, I'm Max Molina." Max was tall and hefty, like a football player. Pointing to a petite woman nearby, he said, "And this is my wife, Minerva. But everyone calls me 'Maxi' and her 'Mini.' Just don't call me Mini and her Maxi!"

Everyone laughed as Max continued. "Again, let me welcome you to Camp Porcupine. Just in case you forget that name, you'll all find a Camp Porcupine T-shirt waiting for you on your bunk. But to make it even easier, you'll see that almost everything around here has been named correspondingly.

"For instance, you've already seen Quill Hill and Porc Palace. The tall trees overhead are a special kind of pine tree called 'Porcu Pines.' Our camp pet is a Vietnamese pot-bellied pig called 'Porc E. Pig.' The barrel behind me is the 'Porc Barrel.' It's full of props for our nightly skits. We'll have daily Bible quizzes called 'Quill Drills.' Plus twice-a-week barbecues called Porc-Outs.'

"Oh, and we don't call that big piece of rock outside, 'Monster Mountain.' We call it 'Porc Peak.' Sunset Lake we call 'Quill Fill.' And to us the waterfall is — that's right, folks — 'Quill Spill.' "

Everyone giggled and groaned at the silly names.

"OK, enough of that! Now for some fun." Max pointed to one side of the room and waved his arm. "Everyone on this side of the room is a Quilly-Billy. Everyone on the other side is a Quilly-Dilly. You have 15 minutes to see how many new Quilly-Billys and Quilly-Dillys you can meet. Ready, set, go!"

When the time was up, Sam had met 27 campers. That's 27 possible new friends, and 27 people to share God's Word with, she thought. That's besides the kids I met at Colleen's table! *Please let this be just the beginning, God*, she prayed. *Maybe tomorrow I'll meet 27 more!*

· Good News · from God's Word

A Widow's Persistence Pays Off
From Luke 18:1-6

Everyone loves a good story. That's why we read books and tell fairy tales and jokes. That's why we watch TV and movies and videos. Even most video games are built around a story!

Jesus told stories, too. He picked subjects with

which His listeners were familiar. It was important that people be able to relate to the meanings. So Jesus often told stories with themes such as gardening, weddings or construction.

One day, Jesus told a story about a poor widow. Because she was poor, she couldn't afford high-priced lawyers. But she needed help. Someone had done something wrong to her — maybe stolen her land or her house — and she needed help getting it back.

Every day, the poor widow visited the judge's court seat. "Justice!" she cried out. "Before God, help me receive justice! That's what judges are supposed to do! Why aren't you helping me?"

But justice was the last thing this judge was interested in. He had plenty of money himself. Why should he bother with her?

Yet every day she came back with her demands.

If she lived today, she'd probably carry a picket sign and be on the evening news! People began talking about her, which embarrassed the judge. Soon they began talking badly about him. "Why doesn't he help her? What kind of judge is he, anyway?" they wondered.

Finally, the judge gave in. Not because his conscience bothered him, but because the woman was so persistent. Jesus says that God also hears His people's persistent prayers and cries for help. And He will help us. But he doesn't help because He's tired of listening to us, like that judge. Instead, God helps us because He loves us.

A Verse to Remember

Even youths grow tired and weary,
and young men stumble and fall;
but those who hope in the Lord
will renew their strength.

— Isaiah 40:30-31

What About You?

Is there something you have tried very hard to do but haven't been able to do yet? Write it here:

_____

Why do you think you haven't achieved it yet? Do you practice enough? Is it something that takes more time or money than you have?

After studying God's Word, do you still think it's something He wants you to do? _____

If it is, write today's date below. Keep trying to achieve it, and keep praying about it.

_____

Quill Drill

Every day at Camp Porcupine the campers have Bible quizzes or "quill drills." Here's a fun one for you about Bible families. Circle the right answer for each Bible girl or woman. You can check your answers on page 191.

1. Eve's husband was:
a. Samson   b. Adam
c. Mark   d. John

2. Eve's father was:
a. Abraham b. Moses   c. Andrew   d. none of these

3. Samuel's mother was:
a. Hannah   b. Anna
c. Huldah   d. Susanna

4. David's wife was:
a. Sarah   b. Abigail c. Naomi   d. Dorcas

5. Jacob's daughter was:
a. Miriam   b. Jezebel c. Elizabeth d. Dinah

6. Mordecai's cousin was:
a. Esther   b. Vashti
c. Rebecca   d. Ruth

7. Ruth's mother-in-law was:
   a. Rachel   b. Leah   c. Naomi   d. Hagar

8. Miriam's brother was:
   a. Moses   b. Aaron   c. both   d. neither

9. Mary's sister was:
   a. Susanna b. Martha c. Anna   d. Deborah

10. Rebekah's husband was:
    a. Jacob   b. Isaac
    c. Elijah   d. Nehemiah

Signs of the Times Puzzle

Add the Secret Letter "U" for "unwavering in faith" to space 4 of the puzzle.

Chapter 16

Looking at Looks

Jenna couldn't believe how much she enjoyed camp – especially considering how much she missed her family! Before she left home, little Noel and Holly had been crawling around and getting into everything. Her mom even had to put special protectors on all the low kitchen and bathroom cabinets to keep them out. She also had to take anything breakable off the living room tables. The Jenkins house was officially child-proof!

"Don't let them grow up while I'm gone," Jenna had begged her mom with a smile.

There seemed to be something to do every minute at camp: cabin clean-up, morning prayer time, breakfast, KP duty, Bible studies, chapel. Then there were a wide range of other activity choices from arts and crafts to music to counseling to every sport imaginable — even in-line skating and scooters! Plus there was a skateboard ramp behind the tennis courts.

And, of course, hiking in the beautiful forest. In the evening, the schedule included more chapel time, singing, skits, games and food. Then the campers headed back to their cabins for quiet time and lights out.

"We must warn everyone," Max said the first morning, "that with the drought we've been having, there is a high fire danger here. So there can be no unauthorized campfires and no playing around with gasoline, mirrors, cap guns or other potentially flammable devices. Any kind of spark can set off a fire. I'm giving everyone a sheet of emergency instructions to follow in case we have a problem. Keep them with you at all times so you know where to go for safety."

Everyone met together for chapel. But Bible studies were held in small groups. Each group studied the topic "Men and Women Who Changed Their World." The first day, Jenna's class studied about beautiful Queen Esther.

Jenna was tall and thin like a model or dancer. But beautiful? She didn't think so, even though her mom did. *But that's what moms are supposed to think*, she decided. *All the PTs are cute or sweet or fun or talented*, Jenna thought. *But beautiful? Brittany, maybe. Not me. Not that I can see anyway.*

After winning her tennis match, Jenna showered and studied her face in the bathroom mirror. Too long, too thin, she concluded. Her nose was too pointed. And look: was that a little pimple on her chin? And her ears stuck out too much. Her camp T-shirt didn't even fit right around her neck.

Jenna felt very discouraged. *How can I ever hope to change my world if I'm not beautiful, the way Esther was?* she thought glumly. Jenna reflected on the skit she had performed for the whole camp earlier that day, when she reached blindfolded into the Porc Barrel and pulled out a mop head. Then she pretended to be a Raggedy  Ann doll pulled by puppet strings. Everyone said they loved it. *But not being beautiful made it even better,* she decided. *None of my talents, like being a good helper and a good friend, can be seen by looking at me.*

That evening during quiet time, Jenna looked up more Bible women, such as Rachel and Rebekah. Rebekah was called "very beautiful" (Gen. 24:16). Rachel was called "lovely in form, and beautiful" (Gen. 29:17). Esther was called "lovely in form and features" (Esther 2:7). *That proves it*, she thought as she shut her Bible.

Just then, Miss Kotter walked into the cabin. "Why, Jenna, how beautiful you look!" she exclaimed.

Jenna looked up from her Bible. "Huh? In these old pajamas? I wish I really were beautiful like Queen Esther. Or even Sam or Brittany. Then God could use me."

Her teacher sat beside Jenna on her bunk bed and hugged her. "Jenna, I saw you out on the tennis court today. You and Maria were both dazzling pictures of strength and grace."

"I'd rather have your brown hair than my blond hair," Sam spoke up from her bunk on the other side of the cabin. "Mine's always stringy and limp."

"I wish I had straight hair like you both," Brittany added. "My curls kink up and then they're impossible to work with."

Miss Kotter laughed. "The truth is, girls, none of us is perfectly satisfied with our looks. But God is. And so are your friends. Because they see the real "you" down inside your looks. We are God's daughters. Whether we're tall like Maria or short like Le. Plump, thin, freckled, dark, light, blond, redheaded, brunette.

"God has made each one of you beautiful. Your job is to take care of the beauty He gave you. And to make sure you grow spiritually and stay beautiful on the inside. That's what made our Bible heroines really beautiful. Not their hairstyles or new dresses. But courage and honesty and kindness and intelligence.

"Now, lights out. Because all of you need your beauty rest!"

· Good News · from God's Word

Here is more about some of the Bible women Jenna studied at camp.

Three Beautiful Women Shine for the Lord

FROM GEN. 24:15-33; 29:1-18; BOOK OF ESTHER

The Bible is full of stories about both men and women. Some were brave, some were cowardly. Some were strong, some were weak. Some were kind, some were cruel.

Queen Jezebel (1 Kings 19:1-2) is one example of a cruel woman. Delilah (Judges 16:4-18) is an example of a beautiful but deceitful woman. Dorcas (Acts 9:36) is an example of loving-kindness. Deborah (Judges 4:4-9) was courageous; so was young Miriam (Exodus 2:7). Mary and Martha (Luke 10:38-39) were faithful and helpful. Naomi (Ruth 4:16) and Ruth (Ruth 1:16) were both loving and hard-working. Hannah (1 Samuel 1:10) was a prayer warrior. Mary Magdalene (Luke 8:2) was grateful. The ideal woman in Proverbs 31 was creative and efficient and well-respected.

We don't know exactly how these women

looked on the outside. But we know how all loving Bible women looked on the inside: like Jesus. That's what the word "Christian" means — "one like Christ."

Most of the Bible women probably had dark hair and eyes like others in their culture. But each of them was beautiful in her own special way, just like you. We're told that Rachel, Rebekah and Queen Esther were all beautiful on the outside. But we know that they were also kind and intelligent. Rebekah and Esther were also very brave. Most admired Bible women had spunk and spark and a love for life. These inner qualities were part of their beauty.

Ask God to help you make your personality a part of your special beauty, too.

A Verse to Remember

Your beauty…should be that of your inner self, the unfading beauty of a gentle and quiet spirit, which is of great worth in God's sight.

— 1 Peter 3:3-4

The Future You

From the list below, select the right word to complete each rhyming line. Believe in what it says!

A. taught   B. see   C. takes   D. scrutiny   E. earn

F. books   G. through   H. be   I. more   J. yield

1. Don't get so caught up in your looks
   That you spend all your time with fashion _____,

2. For there's a whole world to explore —
   Careers, adventures, dreams and _____.

3. Do you know all of history
   And how each country came to _____?

4. Atoms, planets, earth, and sea,
   All ready for your _____.

5. Skyscrapers you might want to build;
   But crops produce a higher _____,

6. Be a pilot or astronaut,
   Or teach to others what you've been _____,

7. Or design hairdos, clothes, or cakes;
   Maybe for racing you've got what it _____.

8. You have an awful lot to learn,
   To study, work at, achieve, and _____.

9. But whatever God leads you to do,
   Do your best; He'll see you _____.

10. Real beauty, you'll then find to be
    God's love shining through for all to _____.

Signs of the Times Puzzle

Add the Secret Letter "E" for "evidence of His spirit" to space 2 of the puzzle.

Chapter 17

Down by the Campfire

It was amazing how much better Jenna felt that night after a hug from her favorite teacher. And the next morning when she walked outside the cabin, the green trees and colorful flowers were so gorgeous, she felt pretty, too.

Everyone had a great time in Bible study that morning. LaToya's group discussed Miriam, one of the Bible women who helped change the world. "It must be great for God to pick you out of thin air and say, 'Here, I need you,' " LaToya sighed.

Miss Temple, her Bible teacher, smiled. "Did God pick her 'out of thin air' and get her ready for Him to use? Or was she already ready, willing and available?"

Already available, the class decided. "And what about you? Are you making yourself available each day for God to use? Or are you saying, 'Wait, God. I have more important stuff to do. This is the time to have fun. I'll let You know when You can use me.' "

LaToya thought more about that during her horseback riding lessons. She thought so hard about it that she started her horse down the wrong trail! But the horse stopped and refused to go until she backed him up and went the right way. The pines provided welcome shade as they rode, but it was still hot. The needles and old leaves underfoot were so dry, they crackled under the horses' hooves.

During arts and crafts, LaToya continued to think about what Miss Temple had said. LaToya was making a felt puppy puppet to use in teaching the kids back home. But she was thinking so hard about God being able to use her, she almost glued its tail to the top of its head!

She thought about it that afternoon down at the lake, too. The water was so wonderful to float in and think. But with her mind a million miles away, she kept floating into other campers, and knocking them under the water!

Finally, LaToya had an idea. She rounded up the Zone 56 praise band members. "Meet me up in the main hall in half an hour," she said. "Ready to practice."

Everyone groaned about leaving the wonderfully cool water, but they showed up at the appointed time. Meanwhile, LaToya asked God to help her. Then she began writing. She had to do a lot of scribbling and erasing, but finally she was done.

"I have a new song for campfire time tonight," she announced.

"Oh, me, too," Josh fired back. "Wait 'til you hear it. 'Buzz, buzz, buzz, the skeeters bomb us,' " he sang off-key to the tune of "Jesus Loves the Little Children."

Everyone laughed. "Well, we'll learn that one, too," LaToya replied. "For fun time. Mine's for get-serious-about-God time. Mine's called, 'Are You Ready?' " She sang the song she made up for them. Soon they were playing and singing along, too.

"Sounds good," Kevin said finally. "Let's ask Max if we can play it tonight around the campfire. Of course that means Brit can't play with us — no plugs for her keyboard."

"That's OK, I can sing along," Brittany decided.

After dinner, KP duty and evening games, everyone headed down to the campfire. Even though it was twilight now, the bare peak of Monder Mountain still glowed rosy from the fading sunset against the backdrop of a very dark cloud.

"Look at that!" Tony cried. "A storm cloud. Maybe we'll get some rain after all."

Max looked thoughtful. "First cloud we've seen here in days, maybe weeks. We sure could use the rain. The lake's way down. Just so we don't get dry lightning strikes! That could change things in a hurry. And not for the good. Everyone, make sure you still have the emergency instructions I gave you in case we need to evacuate."

Flames were already blazing down at the fire ring. "It's not as big as usual," Max explained. "Too much fire danger right now. These trees around you are as dry as tinder. Besides, the evening's too warm for a big fire — and with all this warm Christian fellowship, it's sure to get even warmer!"

One of the high school campers helped lead everyone in silly camp songs. The Zone 56 praise band introduced Josh's song, too. At the last minute, Kevin added ridiculous hand motions to the words. Everyone loved it.

Then Mr. Molina talked to them all about the temptations and problems they face at school. "Even those of you attending Christian schools or home schools aren't immune to problems and temptations," he said. "Problems can find you no matter where you are. Some of you come from broken homes. Some of you may have to worry where your next meal will come from.

"On the other hand, some of your families are well off. Maybe you live in gated communities. Those gates don't keep out problems, either! They don't keep out divorce and loneliness and drugs and alcohol and a feeling of no hope. They don't keep out sin and going along with the gang and getting your life all messed up.

"But God has an answer to all of that: His Son, Jesus Christ. Jesus died on a cross to give you new life and new hope and love that lasts forever. All you have to do is believe in Him and ask Him to be your Savior."

After that, the Zone 56 praise band introduced LaToya's new song. Because the words were so easy, everyone picked them up quickly. They sang quietly and reverently. That night, several of the campers came forward to pray with counselors and ask Jesus to be their Savior.

"Listen," LaToya whispered to Sara as they headed back up the trail afterward. All around them, crickets chirped, fireflies flashed and pine needles crackled underfoot.

"You mean the crickets?" Sara whispered back.

"No, the angels. They're rejoicing tonight. And I'm rejoicing, too!"

· Good News · from God's Word

LaToya and the Zone 56 praise band did what they could for the Lord. Here are some Bible girls who did, too.

Four Maidens Used by God

From Ex. 2:1-10; 1 Kgs. 1:1-15; 2 Kgs. 5:1-14; Luke 1:26-38

When you think of a Bible "hero," who comes to mind? A huge man with armor and a sword? David with a slingshot? Or a warrior on a rearing horse?

What about a slave girl? Being a slave meant working when you'd rather play. Slaves didn't get to go to school. They weren't able to choose what they wanted to be when they grew up. Slaves weren't always able to serve God the way they wanted.

One such slave girl was Miriam. Yet Miriam helped save her baby brother Moses, and thus helped to free her entire nation.

Another slave girl, who belonged to General Naaman's wife, shared her faith with her master when he was sick. He listened to her and sought one of God's prophets to heal him. She saved her master's life!

Abishag wasn't a slave. But she, too, was available and ready for God to use when He needed her. She was a nurse, so she cared for King David in his old age. She helped him to be well enough to continue to lead their nation and avoid a takeover by another king.

And, of course, there was Mary of Nazareth. Her heart was ready and open to God's Word and His plan. She became the mother of our Lord and Savior, Jesus.

Is God able to use you? God still uses girls and women, as He did in the Bible, who love Him and love to study His Word. God's workers are always eager to help others. They take seriously the talents God has given them.

Are you listening for God's call in your life?

A Verse to Remember

Even a child is known by his actions,
by whether his conduct is pure and right.

— Proverbs 20:11

Are You Ready?

Here is the song LaToya and the others sang around the campfire to the tune of "Are You Sleeping, Brother John?" You and your PTs can sing it, too. The key of F (starting on the F above middle C) is an easy key in which to to sing it and play it. If you accompany it on the guitar, you can play just that one chord through the whole song. Sing the entire song together, or try having a leader sing one phrase, then have everyone else sing the echo.

(leader) *Are you ready*, (echo) *Are you ready*,
For Christ today, for Christ today?
Jesus said He's coming, Jesus said He's coming,
Watch and pray, watch and pray.

He is ready, He is ready
To be your Friend, to be Your Friend,
Master, Lord and Savior, Master, Lord, and Savior,
To the end, to the end.

Are you ready, are you ready
Christ to receive, Christ to receive?
He is here and waiting, He is here and waiting,
Just believe, just believe.

Signs of the Times Puzzle

Add the Secret Letter "A" for "available for God to use" to space 9 of the puzzle.

Chapter 18

I Smell Smoke!

Sara went to sleep that night still treasuring the wonderful campfire memories. Then suddenly in the middle of the night…

CRASH! A horrendous boom of thunder shook the cabin walls. Blinding flashes of lightning filled the air.

Miss Kotter jumped up. All the girls shot up in bed, too.

"Wow, that's a big storm!" Sara said as all the other girls murmured in sleepy, scared surprise. But there was no pounding of drops on the roof. Instead, howling winds blew in the windows, left open for cooling breezes, and everything started flying around the room.

The girls jumped out of their bunks and helped each other close the windows and doors, which instantly made the cabin stuffy and warm. Miss Kotter flicked the light switch so they could see to clean up the floor. But nothing happened. The power was out!

"Just like Winter Camp," Sara groaned.

But unlike the Winter Camp cabins, these more rustic huts didn't have intercoms in them. There was a large speaker outside, but without power it didn't work, either. Miss Kotter turned on her flashlight. Jenna turned on her battery-operated radio.  There was a lot of static, but they could make out the words: "Severe storm warning! Gale force winds headed our way!"

Just then there was a loud banging on the door. "A tree limb!" Le cried. But no, it was Max Molina.

"Everyone up and dressed," he said. "Grab what you can and stick it in your suitcases as quickly as possible. Then come on up to the main building. Be sure to close the cabin's door behind you and leave the windows closed. Partner up and stay together.

Hold hands if you can. This wind is bad enough to knock you down."

If the lightning doesn't knock us down first! Sara grumbled in her mind. But she didn't dare say it out loud. As she packed up her suitcase, she remembered one of the camping safety rules she learned in Girl Scouts: always stay away from tall trees in a thunderstorm. But the only place not near tall trees here was the middle of Sunset Lake!

"What about Sonya Silverhorse?" Miss Kotter asked Max. "She's in a wheelchair."

"Mr. Talley and her dad are already on their way to help her. Now when you leave the cabin, step carefully. Some tree limbs are already breaking off and falling across the trails. And more will probably follow. They're hard to see in the dark. So keep your emergency instructions with you. Don't forget: there are flashlights under every bunk."

Then he rushed off to the next cabin.

"Buddy system, everyone!" Miss Kotter barked. "Got everything together? Jackets on and zipped. Bring your sleeping bags and make sure they are tightly tied. You might be sleeping on the floor somewhere tonight. Then grab the rest of your stuff and let's get going."

Sara didn't think she'd ever been so sleepy. But when she stepped outside, the wind woke her up in a hurry. She grabbed Jenna's backpack strap and tried to stay close without knocking Jenna down. Jenna tried to hold onto the flashlight and bags without stumbling in the dark.

Finally, they all made it up to Porc Palace. All

of the windows were closed. A few large, battery-powered lamps were visible around the room. It was stuffy, but then chilly when the roaring wind slipped in through cracks in the windows and doors.

"Some of the boys went back down to the camp ring to make sure all the embers were out," Max said after they did a roll-call to make sure everyone was safe. "We don't dare take a chance for any live embers to be around in this wind. But they were all out."

"Are there any kids over at the school camp?" Mr. Talley asked.

"Yes. Kids from the year-round schools are there. We're putting together a joint plan for evacuation, should that be necessary. Right now, Mini and the other cooks are getting some hot cocoa and cookies ready in the kitchen, using our old propane stove. I need some volunteers to help clear tree limbs off the parking  lot. Also, someone needs to bring Porc E. Pig and the horses up here so we can get them out to the highway quickly if we need to. The animals won't like moving around in the dark and the wind. The rest of you can stretch out on your bedrolls and snooze for a while, if you want."

Which is what most of them did. Stretch out, that is. Being able to sleep on the hard wood floor was something else entirely. *At least*, Sara thought, *this is a good time to pray.* Especially for her brother

Tony, who'd volunteered to help with the horses.
Finally, all the volunteers were back. Sara finally
found a comfortable spot to curl up with her bedroll.
But just then...

"Smoke! I smell smoke!" someone shouted
Sara sniffed. She could, too!

· Good News · from God's Word

*The campers trusted God to help them in the storm.
Here's a Bible girl who also needed God's help.*

Abishag Trusts God in Time of Trouble

From 1 Kings 1:1–2:25

When King David's men searched throughout
Israel for a girl who was not only young but a trained
nurse, they thought she would be impossible to find.
But in the small town of Shunem they found Abishag,
who fit the bill perfectly.

Abishag was kind, gentle, intelligent and
loving. Apparently the king had pneumonia. He
chilled terribly. But before long, with Abishag's care,
he was over his crisis and feeling much better.

Then another crisis arose. One day while she
was taking care of the king, Queen Bathsheba rushed
into the room. "Your son Adonijah is trying to take
the throne away from the rightful heir, Solomon!" she
cried. "It's because you've been sick. They think
you're too weak to do anything to stop him."

So right then King David ordered Solomon to be crowned. It was done. And now Israel had two kings!

Adonijah was very angry. But he pretended to be sorry. He begged Solomon to forgive him. Solomon did. But Adonijah wasn't through plotting.

Next he came to Queen Bathsheba, Solomon's mother. She was cautious. She hadn't forgotten how he tried to steal the throne.

"I don't want the throne now," he said. "All I want to make me happy is to marry Abishag. Please ask Solomon to give her to me." The queen thought that was very sweet and romantic, so she said yes. But of course everything Adonijah said was a lie.

Now what was Abishag to do? She wasn't a royal princess, just a poor young girl from the countryside. All she could do was ask God to help her.

And He did. When the Queen went to see Solomon, God helped him see right through Adonijah's lies. Abishag didn't have to marry Adonijah after all!

A Verse to Remember

*Don't let anyone look down on you
because you are young, but set an example.*

— 1 Timothy 4:12

What About You?

The Boy Scout motto is "Be prepared." Even in the middle of a fun camp week, the campers had to be ready for sudden emergencies. How prepared are you? Think about what you would do in the following situations. If you don't know, talk it over with your parents.

- Smoke

- Power out

- Someone falls

- Stray dog loose in the yard

- Child begins choking

- Hearing strange sounds in the dark

Signs of the Times Puzzle

Add the Secret Letter "Y" for "young but yielded" to space 15 of the puzzle.

Chapter 19

Stuck Here Forever?

One look outside confirmed their fears. At 3 in the morning, the sky behind Monder Mountain was even redder now than it had been at sunset — a roaring, menacing red. The air was heavy with the stinging, acrid smell of smoke.

"We have a forest fire on our hands, kids,"

Max told them when he returned from his office. "A wildfire fed by the wind storm. I've been in touch with the sheriff and emergency rescue teams from three counties. Also the state forest service. An evacuation plan is underway for everyone from both our camp and the school camp, and the animals."

"Is anyone trying to put the fire out?" someone asked.

"Nothing can be done until daylight. Then we can bring in some planes to help us. There's plenty of water in the lake for them to scoop up and drop. But they can't do it in the dark. Besides, we have to wait for the planes to fly in from downstate."

"Who's coming to rescue us?" someone else asked.

"A convoy of buses is on their way. They might take a little longer than normal because of trees toppled over onto the highway by the windstorm. But they'll be here as soon as possible."

"What about the animals?"

Mr. Molina nodded. "Some farmers and horse ranchers have volunteered to bring in trucks and horse vans. Our camp also has two vans of our own. So that's covered, too."

"But how did the forest fire get started? Did our campfire cause it?"

"We don't exactly know yet, of course. But most likely it was caused by lightning strikes. Now remember, kids, we can have an orderly evacuation here or we can have panic. It's up to each of you. Make sure you have all your gear with you. And pray for those brave volunteers coming to our rescue."

After that, some kids tried to call their parents on their cell phones to let them know they were OK. But the fire cut off the connection. Others listened to their radios for news about the fire. Some prayed, or dozed off.

Still others talked. And they had plenty to say.

"I still think it was our campfire," Sara heard Kyle, one of the campers from Midland, say to the groups of guys seated around him.

"Yeah," Brent agreed. "I bet those guys who said they went back to check it out really didn't."

"Of course, they didn't," José snapped. "They just wanted to be heroes. Now look at the mess they got us into. Who was it, that Tony Fields and those guys from Circleville?"

Sara had had enough. "Shame on you guys!" she cried. "Christians aren't supposed to spread false rumors. Especially not about fellow Christians. Especially not about my brother!"

"Oh, zip it," Kyle spat back. "You weren't there to know for sure, were you? Well, were you?"

Mini Molina heard them. "Guys!" she scolded. "Take it easy! There's nothing wrong with being nervous and scared. But there's a lot wrong with accusing someone of something. Especially an innocent person."

By now Tony was back. Sara filled him in on the dispute. "We did go back to the campfire, guys," Tony told them calmly. "Also, Eddie and Dean and I have just brought the horses and pig up from the corral. And we're going back out to stay with them until they're safely in the vans. So if you want to help, come on. If not, I recommend you keep your crazy ideas to yourselves."

The Midland guys sheepishly began fiddling with their suitcases to keep from looking at Tony. After a quick gulp of water, he strode back out the door.

"Be careful, Tony," Sara called after him.

"Don't worry, kid," he called back with a wave. "God is in control."

But she did worry. So did the others. The cooks fixed them all some sandwiches for an early "breakfast." But the smoke smell was so strong they could hardly taste what they were eating.

Just as they finished eating, the sounds of motors and the glare of headlights filled the hall. A huge cheer rang out — the buses had arrived. The campers lined up with their bags and rushed on board. All except for Tony and his friends. "We're riding in the horse vans," Tony explained to Sara through a bus window. "See you later."

Everyone breathed a sigh of relief. These weren't  school buses. In fact, they were sheriff's department buses that usually hauled prisoners. Now at last they were headed for Circleville, safety and home.

Then as they rolled down the highway, a message crackled over the bus driver's radio: "Stop! The wind has shifted. The fire has jumped the highway and is coming your way. Turn around immediately and head north."

Sara looked anxiously out the window into the eerie red-and-black night. What if the north route was cut off by the fire, too? Were they going to be stuck here in the smoke and flames forever?

And what about Tony?

Oh, please, God, take care of Tony!

· Good News · from God's Word

Tony was falsely accused of something. But he didn't get angry — he just went on doing the right thing. Here's a Bible story about another young man who was falsely accused.

Eunice Is Proud of Her Son

FROM 2 TIMOTHY 2:1-5; ACTS 16:1-4

Eunice was a Jew who loved and worshipped God. But her husband was not Jewish. He was a Greek from Lystra, which is part of Turkey today. Eunice and her husband had a boy named Timothy.

During the time Paul was traveling around through various cities and lands telling about Christ, Eunice heard and believed what he said. So did her mother, Lois. So they began teaching Timothy not just the Bible, but all about Jesus.

One day Timothy believed in Jesus for himself. Even though he was very young, he became a strong

Christian. He shared his faith with everyone. Paul was so impressed with him that he asked Timothy to travel and be a missionary with him. Later, he asked Timothy to be a pastor for the church in Ephesus.

Eunice and Lois were, of course, very proud of Timothy. But some people grumbled about him. How could he be a good pastor if his father wasn't a Christian? Besides that, wasn't he too young? Pastors were supposed to have gray hair!

But Paul told Timothy not to worry. In fact, he wrote Timothy two letters to encourage him. He told him to keep on doing what God asked him to do, even though he was young. Just as God will help you with whatever He calls you to do.

A Verse to Remember

The boys accusing Tony sure thought they were right! But they didn't stop to ask God about it first. That's why this Scripture is important to learn.

All a man's ways seem right to him,
but the Lord weighs the heart.

— Proverbs 21:2

Watch Your Tongue!

Use this tricky secret code to discover three good things to ask yourself before you pass on rumors about someone else — even rumors you're sure must be true because "everyone's saying it." What would you feel like if people were saying those same things about you? The answers are on page 191.

Secret Code

A = Z   B = Y   C = X   D = W   E = V   F = U

G = T   H = S   I = R   J = Q   K = P   L = O

M = N   N = M   O = L   P = K   Q = J   R = I

S = H   T = G   U = F   V = E   W = D   X = C

Y = B   Z = A

Ask yourself

1. Is it G I F V _____?

2. Is it P R M W _____?

3. Is it M V X V H H Z I B _____?

Before You Pass It On…

Read this poem and think twice before you judge someone or gossip!

Mary said something to Mandy
And Mandy said something to Drew.
Drew spread it on to Kylie and Dawn
Plus Lauren and Lucy and Lou.
Allison next heard the story.
Jennifer passed it on, too.
But here is the crime: no one took time
To see if the story was true!
When such things come your way,
Please take the time to say,
"And how do you know this is true?"

Signs of the Times Puzzle

Add the Secret Letter "J" for "just and fair" to space 1 of the puzzle.

Chapter 20

Does God Still Work Miracles?

One by one, the buses slowly turned around on the narrow road and headed north. Behind them — and between them and Circleville, Midland and Summer City — the campers could see a wall of roaring flame. The smoke was strong. Many of the kids were coughing.

Sam stared out into the night. She could see whole pine trees burst into flames, one after another. Meanwhile, since the buses were on the small highway that wound through the hills, it was hard to gain speed. It would take a long time going this direction to get to flat land and safety.

Sam thought of how much fun camp had been up until the windstorm struck. Now their very lives were in danger. What would happen now to her plans for the last three weeks of summer? The county fair? Designing back-to-school clothes? Adopting her little kitten? Being with Petie and her parents? Her upcoming birthday? Would she even live that long? Or would this firestorm shift directions again and kill them all?

And then a remarkable thing happened. One kid reached out a hand to another kid on the bus. That kid reached out to someone else. Soon everyone in the bus was holding at least one other person's hand.

Mr. Talley was on their bus, too. "Let's pray," he said. "Pray that God keeps us and the firefighters safe. Remember, God can work miracles. Feel free to take turns praying, and I'll close."

Many kids prayed — even some of the Midland boys who had accused Tony of not checking the campfire. "Please help Tony and the other guys and the horses get out safely, too," Kyle prayed. Afterward, the kids quietly sang praise songs.

It was almost dawn now. Suddenly, Mr. Talley pointed upward. "Hear that roar, kids? That's the planes arriving to dump water on the fire." As the kids strained to look out the windows, the buses pulled to the side of the road to allow truck caravans to pass. The trucks were full of firefighters.

Then Sam asked, "Mr. Talley, do you think it would be OK if we asked God to make it rain? Then the fire would go out for sure." So everyone prayed again.

By now the buses had reached the crest of the hills and were headed down again. "We're in Spencer County now," the bus driver announced. "We'll be out of the forest soon."

As they left the trees, the campers could see a wide valley before them. But the sky was still dark. "Mr. Talley," Le asked, "if there's no fire in this direction, why is the sky filled with smoke?"

And then she discovered the answer: huge drops splatted on top of the bus. Those were rain clouds she saw, not smoke! God had answered their prayers!

By the time the buses and vans rolled into the small town of Spencer Valley, water was running through the streets. Even so, many people were there to meet them, holding out raincoats and umbrellas to help keep them dry.

"We heard about you on TV," cried one woman, as she helped the kids into the school gymnasium. "Everyone in our church has been praying for you and for the children at the school camp, too."

The gym was full of chairs and tables. And the kids from the other camp! There had made it safely as well.

Volunteers from Spencer Valley busily cooked and served a hot breakfast. A couple of small TVs had been placed around the gym so everyone could catch up on what was happening. Phones were set up in one corner so kids could call home. Reporters were in the gym interviewing some of the kids.

Just then Sam heard a familiar voice. "Oh, thank You, Jesus!"

Sara was jumping up and down and pointing to a TV. The news update showed Tony and his friends as they led the horses off trucks and into a nearby barn.

"More good news!" the announcer continued. "All the campers have been evacuated safely to Spencer Valley. This rainstorm now covers a three-county area and is expected to last until at least tomorrow. The forest fire, which firefighters believe was started by a lightning strike, should be contained quickly now with the help of this storm. Officials predict it will be fully under control by sundown or even sooner."

Sam eventually got her chance to call home. "I love you, Mom," she said. "I love you, Dad. I love you, Petie. Tell Sneezit I love him, too."

"Hey, Sam, it's not fair!" Petie complained. "How come you get all the fun?"

Sam laughed. "I guess God just needs to keep showing me how great He is."

· Good News · from God's Word

When Sam and her friends didn't know what to do, they trusted God to help them. So did the women in this Bible story.

Mary and Martha Trust God
FROM JOHN 11:1-44

Mary and Martha and their brother, Lazarus, were three of Jesus' special friends. He liked to spend time in their home. They enjoyed entertaining Him and His friends. Mary especially enjoyed hearing Him explain God's Word. All three loved Jesus very much.

Then one day Lazarus became very sick. In fact, he was near death. But Jesus was nowhere around. He was with His disciples about 50 miles away. That may not seem far — just an hour's drive today. But it was a long way to walk!

"We need to get word to Him anyway," the sisters decided. "If He can get here in time, He can save Lazarus from dying."

Jesus didn't arrive quickly. Not even when He heard Lazarus was sick! Indeed, by the time He returned to Bethany, where the sisters lived, Lazarus was already dead.

Martha rushed out to meet Him. "Lord," she cried, "if You had been here, he wouldn't have died! But I know that even now God will give You whatever You ask. Because You are God's Son."

When Mary saw Him, she fell at His feet weeping, and repeated what Martha had said.

It wasn't too late for Jesus to do a miracle. He raised Lazarus from the dead. God still does miracles today, too.

A Verse to Remember

Jesus replied: " 'Love the Lord your God with all your heart and with all your soul and with all your mind.' This is the first and greatest commandment. And the second is like it: 'Love your neighbor as yourself.' "

— Matthew 22:37-39

Escaping the Fire

In this maze (turn it sideways), see if you can guide the buses away from Camp Porcupine and down to Spencer Valley. The solution is on page 191.

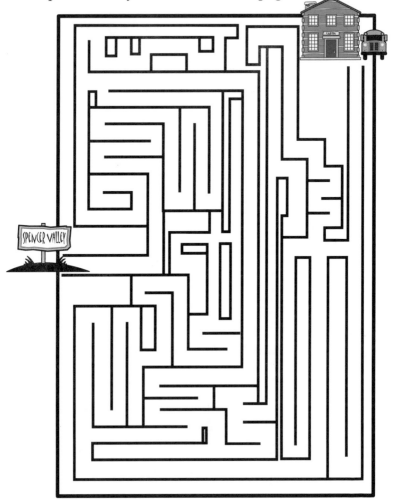

Signs of the Times Puzzle

Add the Secret Letter "O" for "on fire for God" in space 17 to complete the puzzle. Check your answer on page 191.

Glossary (glos/ə rē)

Ahlai: *ah-lie*

Ananias: *an-an-eye-as*

Barabbas: *buh-rah-bus*

Ethiopia: *eeth-ee-oh-pee-ah*

Euodia: *you-oh-dee-ah*

Jarha: *jar-hah*

Lystra: *lis-trah*

Manoah: *man-oh-ah*

Persis: *purr-sis*

Philippi: *fil-ip-pie*

Sapphira: *saf-eye-rah*

Sheshan: *she-shan*

Syntyche: *sin-ti-key*

Tryphena: *try-fee-nah*

Tryphosa: *try-foh-sah*

Vaya con Dios: Go with God

Zeruiah: *zeh-roo-eye-ah*

Zipporah: *zip-poor-ah*

 Answers to Puzzles

Chapter 2
Ric Finds the Lord Maze, p. 34

Chapter 4
Right Side, Wrong Side, pp. 52-53
1. b; 2. b; 3. b; 4. a; 5. b

Chapter 6
Feelings!, pp. 72-73
1. e; 2. f; 3. h; 4. g; 5. a; 6. b; 7. i; 8. c; 9. j; 10. d

Chapter 7
Scat, Cat! Maze, p. 82

Chapter 8
Free to Be Me?, pp. 89-91
1. b; 2. c; 3. d; 4. a; 5. b; 6. c

Chapter 12
Gifts You Can Give
Word Search, pp. 123-124

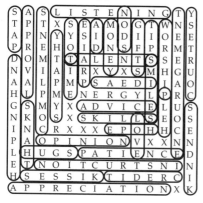

Chapter 13
Working Smart, pp. 131-133
1. b; 2. a; 3. b; 4. a; 5. b; 6. b;
7. b; 8. b; 9. a

Chapter 14
Pet Shop, pp. 141-142
1. J; 2. D; 3. I; 4. G; 5. H; 6. F;
7. B; 8. E; 9. C; 10. A

Chapter 15
Quill Drill, pp. 150-151
1. b; 2. d; 3. a; 4. b; 5. d; 6. a;
7. c; 8. c; 9. b; 10. b

Chapter 16
The Future You, p. 158
1. f; 2. i; 3. h; 4. d; 5. j; 6. a;
7. c; 8. e; 9. g; 10. b

Chapter 19
Watch Your Tongue!,
p. 180
1. Is it TRUE?
2. Is it KIND?
3. Is it NECESSARY?

Chapter 20
Escaping the Fire, p. 188

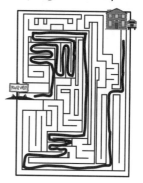

Signs of the Times, p. 26